BIOMIMETICS FOR DESIGNERS

BIOMIMETICS FOR DESIGNERS VERONIKA KAPSALI

Applying Nature's Processes and Materials in the Real World

With 439 illustrations

CONTENTS

ABOVE Macro image showing how the compound eyes of a common fly resemble a geodesic dome structure.

LEFT Biomorphic architecture by architect Nicholas Grimshaw: a covered biome at the Eden Project, Cornwall, UK. The enclosed biomes take the form of self-supporting geodesic structures.

Front view of a jet engine used in commercial aircraft. Visible blades on the fan suck cold air towards an internal secondary fan that compresses the air and slows it down before directing it to the engine.

INTRODUCTION

We live in a time of accelerated technological growth: never before in history has the transition from science fiction to science fact taken place at such pace and scale. Wearable computing and augmented reality are two examples that made the leap from the science-fiction landscape into commercial reality within a relatively short period. However, it is difficult to sustain awe at the marvels of technology and human ingenuity when the outcome of said activity is detrimental to the Earth's geology and ecosystem.

The Covid-19 pandemic highlighted, among other things, the significance and scale of manufacturing issues such as the depletion of the planet's limited, non-replenishing natural resources for fuel and the production of disposable, non-biodegradable materials that end up buried in landfill and or polluting the oceans. We live in a culture of surplus, in which the economic and social value of most everyday products is exceptionally low. Despite warnings from numerous sources, spiralling rates of production and demand show no sign of slowing down; global apparel consumption, for example, is projected to rise by 63 per cent in the next decade, from 62 million tonnes in 2019 to 102 million tonnes in 2030 – equivalent to more than 500 billion additional T-shirts. Many of these garments will be sent to landfill within three years of purchase. As designers, we can no longer take for granted our planet's resources and facilitate current practices of consumption and waste.

　　The purpose of this book is to demonstrate an alternative approach, and the critical role of designers in this trajectory. In the pages to follow, the reader is introduced to example after biological example of how to do as much as possible with minimal resources. Consider the *Apis mellifera*, a simple honey bee that collects pollen from plants to convert into honey for food and wax for hive-building. Wax is an expensive material for a bee; it takes 6 grammes of honey

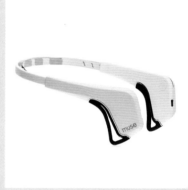

TOP The Muse headset – a wearable device designed to aid in the practice of meditation. The headband features embedded sensors that detect electrical signals generated by different types of brain activity such as thinking, sleeping or relaxing. Data is sent to the wearer's mobile device via Bluetooth, which provides feedback on brain activity.

ABOVE Steve Mann (left), often dubbed the 'father of wearable computing', and his research team at MIT Media Lab demonstrating some of the first wearable prototypes in 1996.

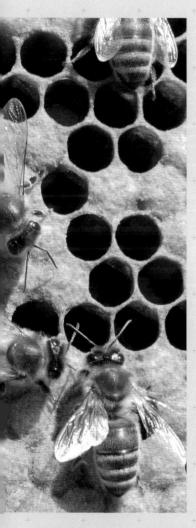

ABOVE Close-up of honey bees at work in a hive. Hive structures are composed of hexagonal wax cells, which are used to store honey and are sealed with a wax layer when full.

to produce 1 gramme of wax and over 4,400 visits to flowers to collect enough nectar to produce a single gramme of honey. This equates to 1 gramme of wax requiring over 26,000 flower visits. The resulting honeycomb structure uses the smallest possible weight of wax to provide the greatest possible storage space with impeccable structural stability.

Just like the honey bee, all organisms in nature must make optimal use of resources, because they are extremely hard to come by. We can learn a lot from biology in terms of how to do as much as possible with as little as possible by understanding how structure (design) is leveraged over substance (materials, elements, monomers and so on) to introduce function and behaviour into material systems. Designers possess the practical skills and knowledge to implement ideas from nature, but lack a framework that enables the translation of design tricks from biology into manufactured structures and products. This book begins to piece together how such a framework might look.

BIOMIMETICS

From Ancient Greek bios, life, and mīmēsis, imitation. The study of the formation, structure, or function of biologically produced substances and materials (as enzymes or silk) and biological mechanisms and processes (as protein synthesis or photosynthesis) especially for the purpose of synthesizing similar products by artificial mechanisms which mimic natural ones.

Webster's Dictionary, 1974

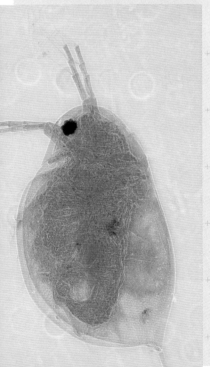

A BRIEF HISTORY OF BIOMIMETICS

English scientist Robert Hooke's 1665 publication *Micrographia* revealed in meticulous detail a previously inaccessible world of life at small scale. With a variety of lenses and optical microscopy, Hooke observed common specimens such as fleas and plant tissue and everyday apparatus including razors and needles, and documented his observations with illustrations. Prior to the development of magnifying lenses and optical microscopes, our understanding of the natural world was limited to what we could experience through observation and basic experimentation using our naked senses. The huge gaps in knowledge were filled with imagination, natural philosophy (the early scientific study of nature) and various belief systems.

As natural philosophy gradually developed into natural science, the equipment and methods used to observe and measure natural phenomena became more sophisticated. Biologists were able to understand how things worked in greater detail using the scientific method. The nineteenth-century English priest John George Wood gave up his curacy to devote himself to writing about natural history. Although not academic, his work was full of energy and enthusiasm, and his voice and ideas were extremely popular with a non-scientific audience. Wood's publications were successful in both Britain and North America, with titles such as *Common objects of the country* and *Field Naturalist's Handbook*. In 1885 he published *Nature's Teachings – Human Invention Anticipated by Nature*, in which he drew upon a lifetime of observations, enthusiasm and love of nature to produce a remarkable account of hundreds of human inventions and how they linked to biological mechanisms that solved the same problem. From rafts and hooks to windows, cameras and electricity, Wood was convinced, by the end of his life, that within nature lay the blueprints for our technological future.

'It is, that as existing human inventions have been anticipated by Nature, so it will surely be found that in Nature lie the prototypes of inventions not yet revealed to man. The great discoverers of the future will, therefore, be those who will look to Nature for Art, Science or Mechanics, instead of taking pride in some new invention, and then find that it existed in Nature for countless centuries.'

J. G. Wood, 1885

BIOPHYSICS AND BEYOND

During the early nineteenth century a small group of scientists began to use physics to explain biological phenomena; this led to the creation of a new discipline known today as biophysics. In the twentieth century, Otto Herbert Schmitt was a brilliant American biophysicist and inventor. As a young researcher, Schmitt applied the physics of electronics to his pioneering study of electrical interactions between nerve endings. By the 1940s he had published several papers on the subject.

Schmitt was part of a generation of scientists who wanted to break out of the boundaries of their discipline and move from specialization to a broader, interdisciplinary mode of working, especially between scientific and technical communities. Like many of his peers, Schmitt felt that the knowledge emerging from biophysics could have a significant impact on innovation, yet there was no existing terminology for what was essentially applied biophysics. Therefore, in 1957 he coined the term **biomimetics** to describe this approach in his doctoral thesis.

In 1958, Major Jack Steele, a doctor at the Wright-Patterson Air Force Base in Dayton, Ohio, used the term **bionics** to define the 'science of systems which have some function copied from nature, or which represent characteristics of natural systems or their analogues'.

In September 1960, the US Air Force Office of Scientific Research (AFOSR) hosted an event titled 'Bionics Symposium – Living Prototypes: the key to new technology' at the Dayton base. Featuring more than thirty speakers from both science and engineering disciplines, the three-day symposium was attended by more than 700 scientists, engineers and military officers. The logo created for the event depicted a linked scalpel and soldering iron, intended to represent the merger of the scientific method with technological application.

Schmitt, who presented a paper at the symposium, disputed the use of the term 'bionic' in his talk, suggesting that it sounded too similar to 'Sputnik' and threatened to offer undue credit for the development of applied biophysics to the Soviets. (Many of the event's papers echoed Cold War tensions, underpinned by a sense of urgent necessity to keep ahead in the race for scientific knowledge and technological innovation.) Schmitt highlighted that although much of the community's focus was on brain functions and computing, it must not lose sight of the myriad other opportunities such as new materials and structures.

> ## 'Bionics, biomimetics, biomimicry, biognosis *all mean the same thing.'*
>
> Professor Julian Vincent

Just as Schmitt had predicted, the term 'bionics' took on a life of its own, especially after science fiction writer Martin Caidin published *Cyborg*, a novel about a pilot who suffers near-fatal injuries while flying an experimental plane. The hero is reconstructed using advanced medical technology, transforming him into a cyborg – a superhuman hybrid between man and machine. The book, published in 1972, went on to form the basis for the cult television series *The Six Million Dollar Man* and subsequently *The Bionic Woman*. The conceptual link between the cyborg and bionics was forged in the popular imagination.

The Bionics Symposium took place for three consecutive years, with much focus on the intersection between biology and electronics or computing. The AFOSR continues today to support pioneering events, exploring and funding research in applied biophysics, with biomimetics high on the agenda.

MODERN BIOMIMETICS

In the early 1970s, two British scientists from very different disciplines began to collaborate at Reading University in the UK. Julian Vincent, a zoologist, and George Jeronimidis, an engineer, worked together on the biomechanics of plants and animals. The pair collaborated on several projects and developed knowledge and expertise in biomaterials such as insect cuticle, mother-of-pearl and wood. Roger Turner, a manager from Imperial Chemical Industries (ICI) who worked on polymers, funded some of their collaborative work. During one of his visits, Turner suggested that the pair should set up a distinct interdisciplinary unit within Reading University that would allow for much better integration between the two disciplines. In 1991, Reading University's Centre for Biomimetics was formed; it would run successfully for nine years. Turner joined the team soon after its launch as the centre's manager, and the group grew to fifteen members of staff. They generated a significant body of pioneering research in areas such as smart materials, food physics, deployable structures, tough biological ceramics and artificial muscles. In 2000, Vincent moved to Bath University to establish the Centre for Biomimetics and Natural Technologies, and the two UK centres carried on until the founders retired around 2008. The two centres are now history, but they had a lasting influence on biomimetics around the world.

Today, biomimetics constitutes an increasingly important multidisciplinary approach to several STEM (science, technology, engineering and mathematics) disciplines. Activity in the academic sector has exploded in the past fifteen years, from 100 journal publications per year in the mid-1990s to more than 3,000 in 2013. In September 2013, England introduced biomimetics into the National Curriculum for Design and Technology for children aged eleven to fourteen; in the rest of the world the subject remains exclusive to engineering undergraduate and postgraduate training and architecture.

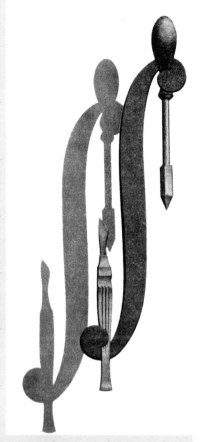

TOP The original logo created for AFOSR's Bionics Symposium in 1960.

ABOVE A micrograph of a common house mosquito wing at 100x magnification – another example of the type of specimen Robert Hooke was looking at.

BELOW Daedalus constructs wings for his son, in a drawing from the German encyclopedia Meyers Lexicon, 1906.

BOTTOM An engraved illustration from the Trousset encyclopedia (1886–91) depicting the Eddystone Lighthouse.

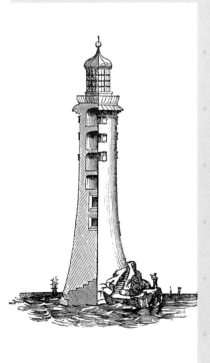

BIOMIMICRY IN MYTH AND REALITY

The sheer beauty, power and magnitude of the natural environment stirs our most primitive emotions and provides a rich source of aesthetic inspiration, as expressed via the arts throughout human history. However, biomimetic innovation has remained relatively undocumented; there is no evidence of biomimetics in great works of art or archaeological findings; even precise terminology to describe biomimetic phenomena was lacking until around the 1950s. Nevertheless, traces of the notion can be found in faint soundbites from the distant past, recorded in myths and legends, or hidden in personal records and diaries. The following are a few examples of biomimetics before it was known as biomimetics – and even in mythology.

DAEDALUS

In Greek mythology, Daedalus was a brilliant architect, sculptor and inventor known for his artistry and skill. He had a nephew named Talus (also known as Perdix) whom he took on as his apprentice. Talus, although very young, demonstrated great inventive talent and was credited for innovations that earned him a reputation to rival his master's. The myth details one particular invention conceived during a walk on the beach where Talus came across the intact spine of a dead fish. Following careful observation, he replicated the structure in metal, thus creating the first saw.

Daedalus grew so jealous of his nephew's talent that one day, he pushed Talus off the Acropolis to his death. As a result, Daedalus was exiled to the island of Crete to serve King Minos. He dreamed of escaping from Crete with his son, Icarus, but Minos controlled the land and sea routes. Inspired by the flight of birds, Daedalus constructed wings of wax and feathers with which to flee the island. The wings successfully carried the pair some distance; however, despite his father's warnings, Icarus flew too high. The heat from the sun softened the wax and caused the wings to fall apart, and Icarus plunged to his death. His father eventually arrived in Sicily.

THE EDDYSTONE LIGHTHOUSE

The Eddystone Lighthouse is located off the coast of Devon in southern England and was built to warn ships of the dangerous Eddystone Rocks on which it stands. The location was subject to such extreme forces from wind and waves that the first two lighthouses on the site, built mainly of wood, did not withstand them for long. Civil engineer John Smeaton was tasked with designing a third structure in the mid-eighteenth century. He modelled its shape on that of an oak tree – wider at the bottom for extra stability – and built it out of granite rather than wood. The lighthouse was completed in 1759 and remained intact for nearly 100 years before it required repairs. The success of the structure was not exclusively due to the radical design of the building: two further innovations that Smeaton pioneered played a significant role. First was the development of hydraulic lime, a form of specialist concrete originally used by the Romans and able to set under water. Second was the use of novel dovetail joints to secure the granite blocks together, resulting in particularly durable masonry. The combination of all these factors resulted in a successful structure that remained in work for more than a century.

THE CRYSTAL PALACE

The giant water lily (*Victoria amazonica*), discovered by Europeans in the early nineteenth century, was long believed to have inspired the design of the Crystal Palace, the home of the 1851 Great Exhibition in London's Hyde Park. However, this is now considered to be something of a myth itself. The first specimens of the tropical plant arrived in Britain in 1847 and were delivered to the horticulturalists at Kew Gardens. The team struggled to create an environment for the plants to survive in, and a seedling was sent to Joseph Paxton, head gardener at Chatsworth House stately home and a talented horticulturalist.

Paxton was also an inventive engineer, who applied his knowledge of botany to further the design of glasshouses. Experimentation with construction methods led him to invent a ridge-and-furrow roof system that enabled the creation of expansive, large-scale structures made entirely of glass and iron. Paxton applied his pioneering system to build the Chatsworth Lily House, an enormous glass enclosure to house the *Victoria amazonica* seedling. His efforts were so successful that in 1849 he produced the first giant lily flowers grown in England.

Paxton drew on his experience of the Lily House construction to propose a highly ambitious building design for the 1851 Great Exhibition. The ideas were well received and he was commissioned as the architect of the Crystal Palace, the world's largest structure built exclusively from iron and glass. After the exhibition, Paxton was invited to give a talk about his design at the Royal Society of Arts, during which he presented an illustration of the *V. amazonica* leaf. It is believed that an overenthusiastic reporter from the audience misunderstood Paxton's talk and generated the myth. Although there are similarities between the structure of the leaf and the ridge-and-furrow system used to construct the Crystal Palace, the system in fact resembles a mechanism closer to other types of leaf such as the beech.

THE EIFFEL TOWER

Another example of early biomimetics is that of the Eiffel Tower, built for the 1889 Universal Exhibition in Paris. French structural engineer Gustave Eiffel was a talented engineer who specialized in the design of large iron structures made from struts and rivets. Iconic examples of his work are the Maria Pia railway bridge (1877) in Porto, Portugal, and the internal framework for Frédéric Auguste Bartholdi's Statue of Liberty in New York (1884).

For his tower, it is believed that Eiffel was inspired by the collaborative work of German anatomist Hermann von Meyer, whose study of the human femur (thigh bone) revealed an internal structure of crisscrossing fibres called trabeculae, and Swiss engineer Karl Culmann, who created a mathematical model of these fibres, describing them as being like the struts and braces used in buildings.

The original design for the Eiffel Tower was actually conceived by two of Eiffel's employees, Maurie Koechlin, a Swiss engineer who had studied under Culmann, and the French engineer Émile Nouguier, in 1884. Gustave Eiffel perfected the tower's design by drawing on his expertise with large metal structures to calculate the curve of the base pylons required to resist wind load. The resulting 324-metre (1063-foot) iron structure was constructed as the centrepiece for the 1889 exhibition and has become one of the most iconic buildings in history.

CAT'S EYES

Reflective road studs, or cat's eyes, are one of the most significant innovations in road safety, invented in 1933 by Percy Shaw of Halifax, England. Shaw was a brilliant inventor and entrepreneur; as a schoolboy he developed a process to back carpets with rubber and devised a method for pumping petrol. By the age of forty, he was running a business repairing roads and garden paths with tarmac, and invented a mechanical pavement roller to facilitate his work.

At the time, many motorists had come to rely on the reflection of their headlights off the smooth metal surface of tramlines for guidance when driving at night. As cars and buses replaced trams, the tramlines were gradually removed, and Shaw realized the need for a reflective surface for night traffic. Shaw's inspiration for the cat's-eye device is believed to have been in part the piercing eyeshine of cats' eyes in the dark and fog, and in part the reflective road-sign technology invented by Richard Hollins Murray from Herefordshire six years previously. Shaw spent some time perfecting his device, but essentially built on the known optical properties of reflecting lenses; his contribution was to work out how to mount these in a robust, practical housing and to establish a cost-effective method of mass production.

ABOVE Close up of a cat's eye. Many animals, including the cat, have a layer of tissue behind the retina known as the *tapetum lucidum* that reflects light back through the eye. As well as aiding in their night vision, it results in 'eyeshine', the characteristic glow when the animal's eyes are caught in the light.

RIGHT A road stud with yellow reflector.

BIOMIMETIC DESIGN

The silos in which the STEM (science, technology, engineering and mathematics) and creative communities operate have begun to break down; the interaction between disciplines echoes that among the scientific and technical communities that occurred in the 1950s. Creative and STEM collaboration has opened up an exciting new landscape populated by scientists and engineers working with artists and designers hungry to cooperate with one another. Increasingly, the STEM community has begun to realize the importance of creative input at the early stages of innovation rather than at the end, although this new dynamic is in its infancy.

Current design/art/science collaborations vary greatly in scale and output, from inquisitive hobbyists who transform domestic spaces into makeshift labs to artists specialized in unconventional bio-based media aiming to challenge the status quo and stimulate debate. For example, Anna Dumitriu is a British artist whose media include live bacteria, robotics and textiles and who makes work at the borders of art and science, often aimed at raising awareness of the impact antibiotics have on bacteria and public health. Her latest solo exhibition (2014), titled 'The Romantic Disease: An Artistic Investigation of Tuberculosis', is an investigation into humankind's strange relationship with this disease, from the early superstitions surrounding it, through the advances in antibiotics, to the latest research into the genome sequencing of bacteria. Dumitriu embeds herself in the labs of the microbiologists she collaborates with; her presence transforms the space into a studio/lab hybrid that grants her access to a range of unconventional techniques, including genome sequencing.

Like Dumitriu, many pioneering artists and designers are moving away from conventional materials, methods and workspaces to explore new territories in biology, engineering and science. The drivers vary – from curiosity and provocation to grand challenges such as sustainable manufacturing. It is without doubt that we inhabit an age where boundaries between creativity and science have been irrevocably blurred.

Nature shows us how to achieve advanced, complex systems and structures that form closed networks of interdependent relationships and feedback systems by combining simple materials with 'clever design' using minimal resources. This approach to design is strongly aligned to many of the technical challenges faced by the engineering community; the relevance to the creative design sector is less obvious. In fact, a review of this approach for the creative design sectors generates a paradox.

ABOVE Gaudí's Sagrada Família church in Barcelona, Spain, is an example of biomorphic architecture.

BELOW *Genius Germ* (detail, below left), part of Anna Dumitriu's 'Romantic Disease' series, 2014. The piece was inspired by Pablo Picasso's work *Pobres genios!* (1899–1900).

If biomimetics has no intentional or direct impact on the aesthetic aspects of design, instead focusing on the transfer of functional properties of biological mechanisms into technology, what is its relevance to the design community?

This book aims to unravel this paradox by exploring the key biomimetic principles in the context of creative design. Biomimetics is a young discipline, and the definition of its principles and practice has been the topic of significant debate within the biomimetic communities in recent years. Initiatives from both biomimetic and design communities have produced numerous manifestos describing key principles and methodologies deduced from existing practice, coupled with tools that offer guidance in biomimetic thinking, project management and design. Although the manifestations of this work vary, there are a number of key recurring principles (the following descriptions are representative and not exhaustive).

MAXIMIZE RESOURCES
This is one of the most fundamental principles underpinning what we perceive as 'clever design' in biology. Resources in the natural environment are limited; plants and animals have to compete to gain access to vital nutrients. Essential amino acids, for example, are complex protein molecules that are not produced by the body, and thus can be accessed only from external sources. These need to be found and consumed on a regular basis to maintain health; humans access these in abundance as consumers of the food industry, while animals need to source them from their local environments, where resources are often limited and in demand by several species. It is therefore imperative that resources obtained by an organism are put to the best possible use. Shape and structure in biology are very efficient vehicles for maximizing the use of resources; there are numerous examples in biological systems where a combination of structural features and behaviour can enable a particular organism to do more with less. Humpback whales and boxfish are just two examples featured in this book of performance-enhancing shapes that enable motion using modest amounts of energy, while honeycomb and abalone shells are examples of super-strong structures built from small amounts of abundant and inherently weak materials.

USE FREE OR ABUNDANT ENERGY SOURCES
Animals spend most of their time looking for food; systems that take advantage of free or abundant energy sources, such as sunlight, are numerous in nature. This book features several examples of harvesting unconventional energy sources that challenge our dependence on electricity and

petrochemicals, such as extracting water from thin air and harnessing environmental moisture or temperature to power motion.

BE MULTIFUNCTIONAL
There are not many examples of things in biological systems that perform only a single function. Seed pods, for instance, provide a protective environment that allows the seed to grow, and once matured the pod or casing transforms into a transportation and dissemination management device. The specialized ribbed design of the surface of sharks not only minimizes drag forces created by water but also acts as an anti-adhesive that prevents microorganisms from sticking to the skin.

WASTE EQUALS RESOURCE
The Earth is a closed system – aside from meteorites impacting the planet, there is no way of introducing new matter to the system or of taking it away. In the natural world, these finite resources are of great value and nothing goes to waste. This is in direct contrast to the reality of our man-made environments, and the source of one of the key global challenges facing future generations. Biology can show us how to create information-rich materials with specific properties using abundant resources from waste streams as an alternative to landfill.

LOCALIZE SENSING AND ADAPTATION
Organisms in nature live in symbiosis with the environment yet are autonomous; they are able to sense and respond to changes in their habitats, communicate, heal, grow and replicate. These behaviours are incredibly complex, yet understanding them and reinterpreting them into man-made systems is one of the most exciting and cutting-edge areas of biomimetic innovation today. Most of these developments – such as programmable materials, self-assembling robots and swarms of connected devices – still reside in labs, but gradual introduction of these technologies into consumer goods is not as far off as we might think.

BELOW A geodesic dome is a spherical structure whose characteristic lattice shell is formed of intersecting triangular elements. Often this type of structure is referred to as biomimetic thanks to its aesthetic qualities.

BOTTOM A series of vases in biomorphic designs.

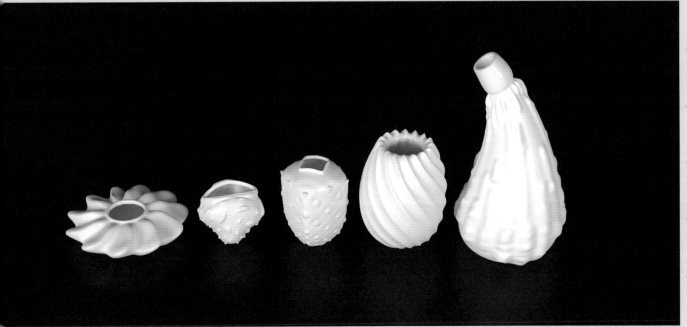

THE FUTURE

The Internet of Things (IoT) is today's prevailing 'grand narrative' of innovation; it describes the current direction of technology in terms of products and services. IoT depicts a vision of the future where smart products, services and environments form dynamic interconnections with the individual. Currently 'unconnected' technologies such as showers, clothes, washing machines and cars will evolve new, intelligent functionalities that enable information flow through sensing and actuation. The IoT proposition suggests a paradigm shift from static unconnected environments to what is essentially a biological ecosystem of components based on the biomimetic principle of localized sensing and adaptation.

The possibilities presented by advanced materials shatter the boundaries of our current understanding of the 'object' as inanimate and usher us into a new era of intelligent, connected products, surfaces and systems. This emerging landscape offers opportunities for a new breed of designer to create a future with a novel set of tools; however, an engaged creative community is also responsible for the direction and application of these new technologies in a way that will most benefit humanity. Just as Schmitt argued in 1960, we must not look backwards in order to progress technology. The merging of existing devices and products offers limited scope – do we really want our phones integrated into our garments? Instead, we must identify needs emerging from a world presented with numerous global challenges such as an ageing population, dependence on depleting energy sources, and population growth. There is much we can learn as designers from nature's lean operation.

ABOVE View of Lujiazui financial district in Shanghai including the Shanghai Tower, China's tallest building. Shanghai is home to cutting-edge buildings that explore what our future cities will be like. The scope for a biomimetic approach to the design and planning of the future of our built environments is truly exciting.

OPPOSITE An example of biomorphic façade design. Architectural second skins can have a transformative impact on the appearance of a building as well as offering standard functions such as fire resistance. They also present a promising platform for future biomimetic innovation.

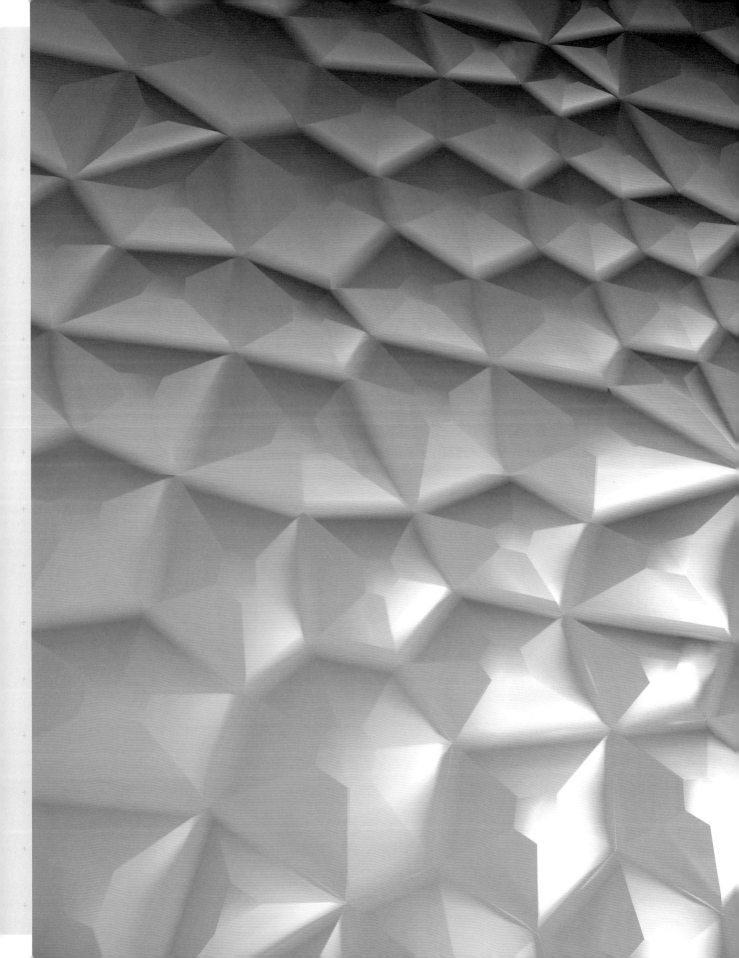

01

BIOLOGY

SHAPE

BIOMIMETIC APPLICATION

OPPOSITE Hawk-wing detail. Bird
wings present a significant biomimetic
paradigm: although key to bird flight,
they signify the complexity of technology
transfer from biological systems,
representing the balance between an
in-depth understanding of the relationship
between design and behaviour and the
practical approach.

This chapter explores the way in
which form in biology supports the
optimization of resources and how
it has inspired the design of pivotal
products and technological innovation.
Biology shows us not only that
shape can introduce multiple passive
functions to a system, but also that
it is a powerful factor in energy
management during movement
through air or water.

This section also begins to
unpack the profile of the biomimetic
practitioner and reveals that biomimetic
design is not exclusive to engineering.
The following case studies describe
innovations by creative individuals
who are not necessarily scientists or
engineers but who have demonstrated
an extraordinary ability for abstraction
from biology and for the synthesis of
novel, solution-based concepts using
known technologies.

HEDGE THORNS | BARBED WIRE

Naturally spiky barriers | Efficient spiked fencing

LEFT A typical unfenced landscape of the American West, c.1881.

ABOVE Detail of thorns in a hedgerow, forming an effective barrier.

Native American Indians were the principal inhabitants of the North American Western territories until the mass migration of Americans sparked by the Homestead Act signed by Abraham Lincoln in 1862. Settlers were entitled to ownership of 65 hectares (160 acres) of public land in exchange for a small fee as long as they resided on the land for five years. Over a period spanning several decades, many migrated from the East to the West, seeking opportunities in the 'new land'. This new community of landowners shared a need to define the boundaries of their vast estates, both to mark their territory and to protect harvests and livestock. The landscape itself was vast, flat and monotonous. This treeless terrain of open prairies offered little in terms of traditional

fencing materials such as wood and stone. Many landowners planted the native Osage orange trees along sections of their property borders, thus creating thorny hedgerows that grew into robust barriers (some original hedgerows survive today), while the characteristic thorns provided an excellent deterrent for both livestock and wild animals. Nevertheless, fencing estates of this scale was a monumental task, and a desperate need emerged for a cheaper solution that was quick and easy to assemble. The problem was not exclusive to the Western territories; by the end of the Civil War (1861–65), Southern landowners, who had historically relied heavily on slave labour for the upkeep of their estates, were also in urgent need of a simple and cost-effective alternative.

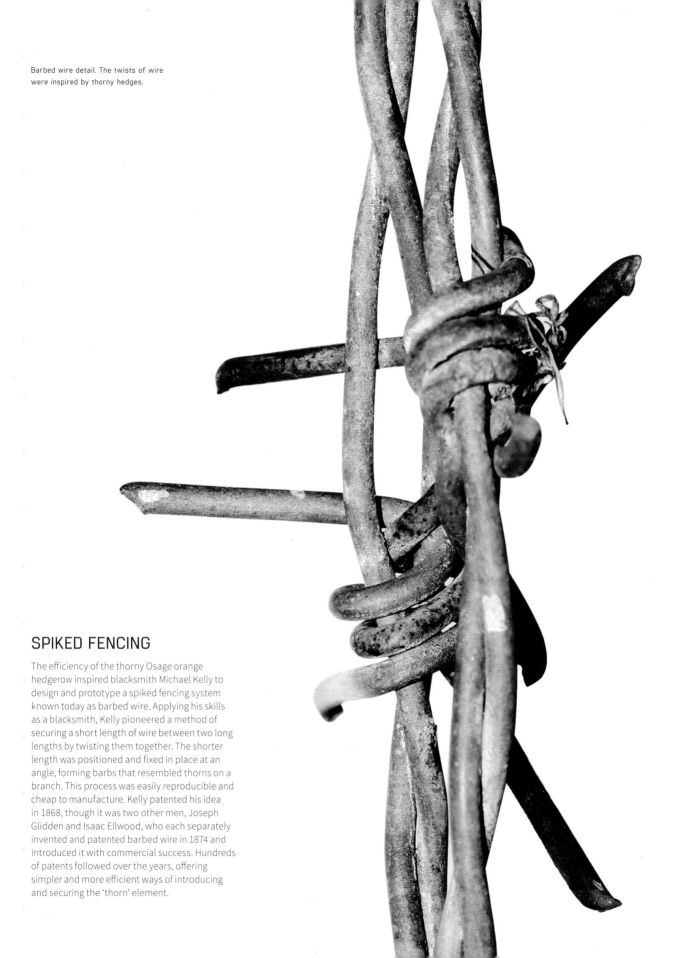

Barbed wire detail. The twists of wire were inspired by thorny hedges.

SPIKED FENCING

The efficiency of the thorny Osage orange hedgerow inspired blacksmith Michael Kelly to design and prototype a spiked fencing system known today as barbed wire. Applying his skills as a blacksmith, Kelly pioneered a method of securing a short length of wire between two long lengths by twisting them together. The shorter length was positioned and fixed in place at an angle, forming barbs that resembled thorns on a branch. This process was easily reproducible and cheap to manufacture. Kelly patented his idea in 1868, though it was two other men, Joseph Glidden and Isaac Ellwood, who each separately invented and patented barbed wire in 1874 and introduced it with commercial success. Hundreds of patents followed over the years, offering simpler and more efficient ways of introducing and securing the 'thorn' element.

TIMBER BEETLE
MANDIBLES

Specialized wood-shredding

MODERN
SAW CHAIN

Revolutionary metal saw chain

Logging is one of the world's deadliest jobs, responsible for more deaths at work than any other occupation. In the early days of commercial-scale logging, tree-felling was mainly conducted using handsaws, a process that was inefficient, dangerous and labour-intensive. The industry was desperate for a tool that would make the work easier and safer. The first patent for a petrol-powered saw with an endless chain was granted to Harvey Brown from New York in 1858. However, this saw failed to take off as it – and many subsequent improvements to the design by fellow inventors – lacked safety and reliability.

In the 1940s Joseph Buford Cox, a trained welder, moved to Oregon with his brother to work in the lucrative logging industry. Cox was aware of the industry's need for mechanization and was asked to try out an early wheel-mounted power stump saw driven by a motorcycle engine. He soon concluded that the mechanism, and especially the design of the chain, was hugely inefficient. Determined to find a better solution, Cox was convinced that the answer would be found in nature.

LEFT A timber beetle larva shredding a section of log.

BELOW Logs piled by the side of a forest road ready for transport.

ABOVE A common chainsaw.

RIGHT During modern tree-felling, workers use protective clothing and guarded chainsaws.

BELOW A detail of the chain shows the C-shaped links inspired by the timber beetle larva's mandibles.

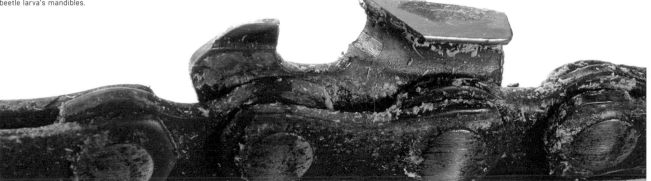

FROM MANDIBLE TO SAW

The larvae of the timber beetle *Ergates spiculatus*, known as the 'pine sawyer', is an infamous pest that turns wood into sawdust. While cutting timber one day, Cox stumbled across a nest of timber beetle larvae and wondered: how do they do it? Using nothing more sophisticated than a magnifying glass, he observed the grubs for hours and noticed that the highly efficient cutting mechanism was achieved by a combination of behavioural and structural features. The larvae used two specialized sharp mandibles in a side-to-side movement, cutting into the wood from an angle. This was very different from the approach used by loggers, which involved moving the handsaw backwards and forwards in a scratching motion across the grain of the wood.

Cox combined his knowledge of welding with the insight he had gained from his observations of the beetle larvae, and developed a C-shaped chain design that imitated the structure and technique of the larvae. The design was patented in 1947 and Cox set up the Oregon Saw Chain Manufacturing Corporation, which still holds a strong position in the market today.

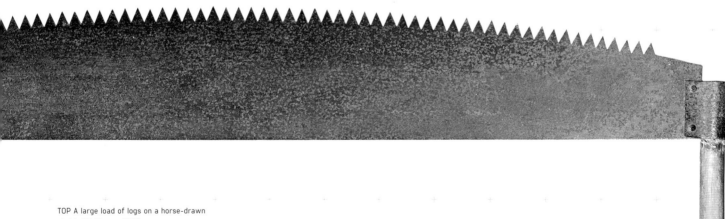

TOP A large load of logs on a horse-drawn sled in Michigan, c.1899.

ABOVE A handsaw blade.

RIGHT Sorting logs on the water.

BELOW A professional lumberjack
using a modern chainsaw.

BIRD FLIGHT

Avian locomotion

MODERN AVIATION

Artificial flight

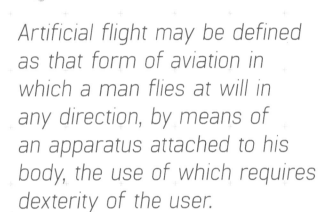

Artificial flight may be defined as that form of aviation in which a man flies at will in any direction, by means of an apparatus attached to his body, the use of which requires dexterity of the user.

Otto Lilienthal, 1895

Superhuman characters with the ability to fly like a bird inhabit the mythical narratives of civilizations across time, from Hermes with his magic sandals and Isis with her kite-hawk wings to the more recent Superman of our own culture. Attempts to design apparatus that would allow humans to imitate the flight of birds through technology rather than magical or spiritual means are not exclusively a modern phenomenon, but it is relatively recently that flight has become a reality for human beings.

LEFT A zebra finch in flight.

BELOW A competitor taking part in a hang-gliding competition on Klementieva Mountain, Ukraine, in 2012.

Otto Lilienthal flying the two-surface glider in which he made scientifically documented sustained flights in the early 1890s.

ABOVE Orville Wright in the Wright brothers' powered plane, *c*.1908

BELOW A brahminy kite in flight. Birds' wings are adapted for different requirements, from flapping and hovering to gliding and soaring.

Bird aviation is enabled by a combination of structural and behavioural characteristics such as wing flapping and gliding via wing extension. English engineer Sir George Cayley, often called the 'father of aviation', was the first scientist to understand the aerodynamics of flight (the interplay of weight, drag, lift and thrust forces). In 1799, Cayley articulated the first concept of a modern piloted aircraft that was heavier than air, with fixed wings and separate systems for lift, propulsion and control. He dedicated much of his life to the design and development of gliders.

WING SHAPES AND ANGLES

Otto Lilienthal, a German civil engineer, conducted one of the first studies of bird wing shapes around 1890. Convinced that the key to the gliding behaviour in birds was the wing curvature, he applied his findings to the design and development of specialized wings with curved cross-sections (aerofoils) for his gliders. Lilienthal's work resulted in the invention of the first safe hang-gliders capable of multiple journeys.

Lilienthal's gliders relied on shifting body weight to manage the direction of travel. Some years later, the Wright brothers, Orville and Wilbur, considered this a significant limitation and set out to develop a method for controlling the direction of flight with greater accuracy. Drawing on the work of Cayley and Lilienthal, as well as on the flight studies made in the fifteenth–sixteenth centuries by Leonardo da Vinci, the brothers studied the way birds manoeuvre during flight and discovered that they manage direction by altering the angle of their wings. This finding formed the basis of the Wrights' wing warping technology – a mechanism consisting of a rudder-controlled system. They applied this mechanism to the design of controversial gliders whose wings were not fixed but controlled by a pulley system that allowed them to alter the direction of flight by warping or twisting the wings, just like birds.

ABOVE LEFT Detail of a bird wing, showing the 'covert' feathers, which help to create smooth airflow over the wind.

ABOVE An osprey in flight, showing the complex system of specialized feathers designed to enable flight, including the long, stiff *Pennae volatus* (flight feathers) located on the end of the wing and tail.

RIGHT A northern cardinal with extended wings, revealing both primary (tip of wing) and secondary flight feathers.

ABOVE A plane preparing for takeoff on an airport runway.

RIGHT Detail of a plane wing. The three-axis control system invented by the Wright brothers that allows the pilot to steer the aircraft effectively remains the standard on fixed-wing aircraft today.

KINGFISHER BEAK

Splashless diving

SHINKANSEN BULLET TRAIN

Reduced noise, efficient energy consumption

The Sanyo Shinkansen is a line of the Japanese high-speed rail network, connecting Osaka to Fukuoka with electrically powered trains dubbed 'bullet trains' in English because of the breakneck speeds they can achieve. The 500 series of Shinkansen trains is designed to reach speeds of 320 km/h (200 mph), making it one of the fastest trains in the world. The train line consists of both open track and enclosed tunnels. During trial runs, the train caused a tremendous sonic boom as it exited the tunnels at top speed. The difference in air pressure between the open and covered sections created waves that shook the carriages as the train travelled through the tunnel. These waves reached the speed of sound when exiting the tunnel, thus causing the earsplitting

ABOVE A kingfisher in flight preparing to dive.

LEFT The kingfisher's long, streamlined beak forms a wedge shape with its head that is round in cross-section and has a pointed tip with grooves along each side, allowing it to dive into the water without making a splash.

noise, which was heard by residents living as far as 500 metres (1,640 feet) from the track. With sound levels exceeding environmental standards, the 500 series would be limited to the speed of the previous version and unable to accelerate to full capacity.

The engineering team, led by German industrial designer Alexander Neumeister, realized that they needed to find a way to smooth the transition from areas of low to high pressure and looked to biology for ideas. One of the team members, a keen birdwatcher, suggested the kingfisher as a potential model. The bird lives near rivers and feeds on fish that it catches by diving from the air (area of low resistance) into water (higher resistance) without causing a splash – a feat enabled by the unique shape of its beak.

A POINTED NOSECONE

The team conducted a series of experiments that involved shooting various bullet shapes into a pipe and measuring the waves produced. They were able to calculate a model for the ideal shape using advanced computing and data analysis from experiments. The design produced by CAD proved identical to that of the structure of the kingfisher's beak. The outcome of this work informed the shape of the forefront of the 500 series train, which has a nosecone 15 metres (49 feet) long with a nearly round cross-section. This design achieved a 30 per cent reduction in air pressure during entry into tunnels compared to its predecessor, reducing turbulence and improving the smoothness of the ride as well as reducing the noise created on exit from tunnels. It also uses 15 per cent less electricity even at higher speeds when compared to the former series.

A Shinkansen train at Okayama station in 2014. The 500 series Shinkansen is operated by the West Japan Railway company on the Sanyo line at a speed of up to 285 km/h (180 mph).

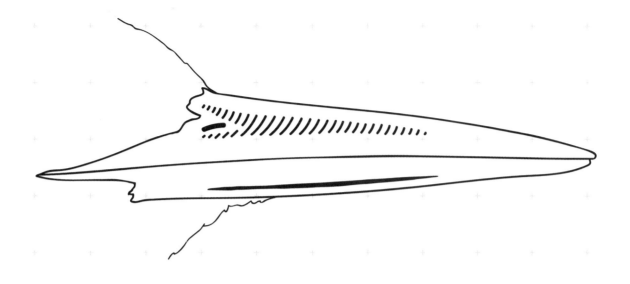

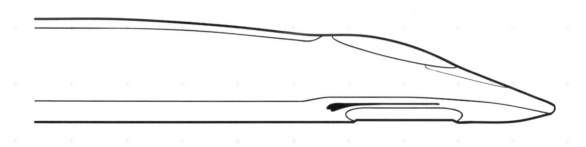

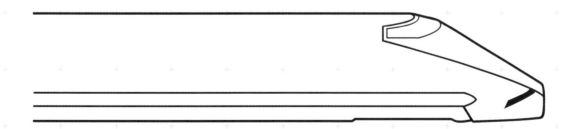

TOP Illustration of a kingfisher beak.

CENTRE Illustration of a Shinkansen 500 series train.

ABOVE Illustration of a Shinkansen 300 series train.

OPPOSITE A white-throated kingfisher perching on a branch.

DOLPHIN BODY SHAPE

Energy-efficient swimming

STREAMLINED VESSELS

Fusiform design

Earth's lakes, rivers and oceans conceal a vast variety of specialized shapes, structures and behaviours that have evolved to enable plants and animals to survive in aquatic environments. Movement through water is an energy-hungry process, as it can occur only when momentum from the animal is transferred to the aquatic environment. Compared to air, water is a dense and viscous medium, able to generate significant resistive forces such as drag. The friction between the surface of a moving body and the contacting layer of water causes a reduction in the speed of flow: as water flows over a surface it slows down, and drag is created by the difference in speed between the sheet of water that comes into contact with the object and the water flowing away.

Energy produced by aquatic animals is consumed in the production of adequate thrust to move forward and overcome drag forces. The efficient management of this energy loss determines an animal's performance in terms of speed, acceleration and manoeuvrability. Strategies that maximize the control of water flow are essential to the survival of a particular species and are believed to be subject to strong evolutionary selection pressures. As a result, many unique and clever systems have evolved to allow optimized energy use by managing water flow, reducing resistive forces and increasing propulsive forces.

Wild dolphins swimming underwater and leaping out of it, showing their highly streamlined shape.

ABOVE The launch of the USS *Albacore*
(AGSS-569) on 1 August 1953.

BELOW Illustration of dolphin fusiform
body and the characteristic elongated
droplet shape.

STREAMLINED HULLS

Marine mammals such as dolphins and whales
characteristically migrate long distances and are
apex predators. The primary strategy for drag
reduction in aquatic mammals is the streamlined
profile of their bodies and appendages. This was
first discovered around 1800 by the aerodynamics
pioneer Sir George Cayley, who studied the
body shape of a dolphin and concluded that
the fusiform design – resembling an elongated
droplet with a rounded leading tip and a thick
middle tapering gradually to the tail – delivered
the least resistance among solid shapes. Aquatic
animal body parts such as fins, flippers and tails,
similarly, echo this design principle. Cayley's
findings inspired the design of modern submarine
hulls, such as the research submarine the USS
Albacore in 1953.

HUMPBACK WHALE PECTORAL FIN

Precision manoeuvrability in water

APPLIED TUBERCLE SYSTEMS

Improved efficiency in air and water

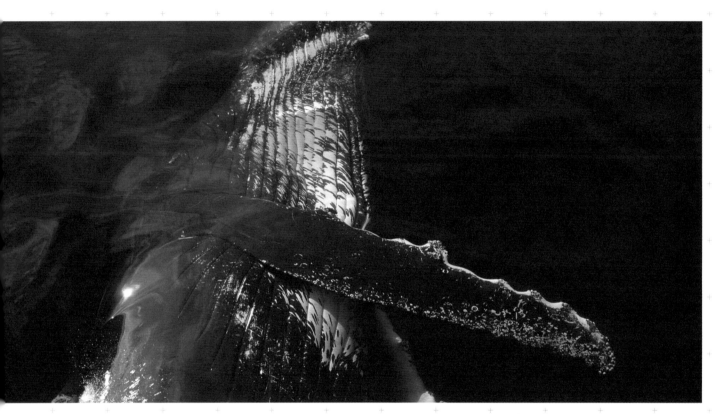

ABOVE Side view of a humpback whale and pectoral fin, showing the bumps, or tubercles, along one edge of the fin.

RIGHT A humpback whale manoeuvring outside water (breaching).

An adult humpback whale (*Megaptera novaeangliae*) can grow to 15 metres (50 feet) long and weigh 40 tons, yet is capable of precise and agile manoeuvres that support behaviours essential to its survival. For example, the humpback can swim in tight circles as narrow as 1.5 metres (5 feet) in diameter, which generates vortices filled with bubbles that trap large quantities of krill in a single session.

The level of agility demonstrated by such a large creature suggests a highly sophisticated method of controlling and manipulating the drag

forces generated during movement in the water.
Scientists discovered that this extraordinary
behaviour was made possible simply by the
design of the pectoral flipper. The flipper is
long with a high aspect ratio – that is, there is
a large difference between the length and the
width of the structure – similar to a bird's wing.
Characteristic large irregular bumps called
tubercles line the flipper's leading edge. As the
flipper moves, the tubercles manage the flow
of water by splitting the contacting sheet of
water into even channels. This simple design
feature is estimated to improve lift by 8 per cent
and reduce drag by 32 per cent when compared
to a smooth flipper.

TUBERCLE TECHNOLOGY

Dr Phil Watts and Dr Frank Fish are leading
experts and pioneers in the study of humpback
whale flippers. In 2004 they founded WhalePower
to commercialize biomimetic design based
on their observations and branded it Tubercle
Technology. Although the application landscape
for this kind of technology is vast, the team
focused on improving the efficiency of wind
turbines. The first commercial application
produced by WhalePower was a specialized
wind turbine blade able to generate more energy
at moderate wind speeds than a conventional
blade. WhalePower is currently developing
smaller blades for application in fans, which
are estimated to require 20 per cent less energy
to operate.

TOP, LEFT AND RIGHT A modern wind
farm, and detail of a conventional
wind turbine blade.

RIGHT, TOP TO BOTTOM A large sheet of
water flowing over the smooth surface
of a fin creates a strong drag force. Water
flowing over a bumpy fin is divided into
smaller streams, minimizing the creation
of drag forces. A tubercle turbine blade
featuring the bumpy edge inspired by
the design of the humpback whale fin.

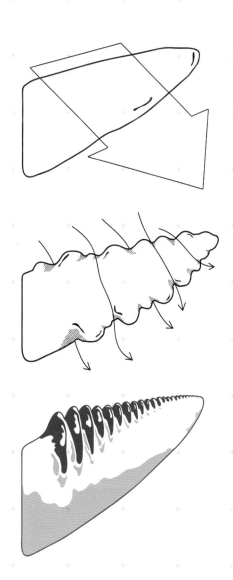

TUBERCLE SURF FINS

Originally trained in philosophy, Roy Stuart is a New Zealand-based surfboard shaper who has honed his craft over twenty years. He is known for creating the world's most expensive surfboard, the handcrafted wooden 'Rampant', which he sold for more than a million dollars. Stuart is also an ingenious innovator who realized that if he applied the principles of Frank Fish's Tubercle Technology to the design of a surfboard fin he would be able to improve the performance of large-wave surfboards during contact with water. Following a period of experimentation, Stuart successfully developed a new class of surf fin that features tubercle-type ridges along the leading edge. Surfers testing the new design claim that the Warp Drive Bumpy Leading Edge Fin (BLEF), positioned at the tail end of the bottom of the board, had a great impact on manoeuvrability, control and lift when compared to conventional designs.

Initially, BLEF designs were applied exclusively to Stuart's handcrafted wooden fins: this provided excellent results, but each fin could take up to sixty hours to make. Recent advances in additive manufacturing (3D printing) have enabled lightweight polymer versions to be easily and inexpensively produced. Stuart's team also plans to mass-produce fins using CNC-cut fibreglass panels, facilitated by computer-aided design that enables accurate reproduction of tubercule design.

ABOVE The humpback whale's tail is serrated and pointed at the tips.

ABOVE Roy Stuart with a surfboard prototype featuring 3D-printed tubercle-inspired surf fin.

ABOVE RIGHT Detail of a handcrafted wood surfboard with tubercle-inspired fin.

It's analogous to having tyres with tread, rather than bald ones.

Roy Stuart

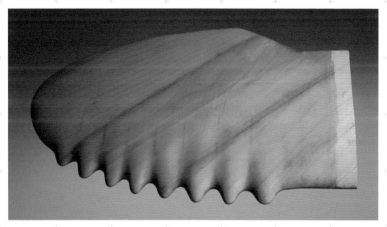

ABOVE Wooden handcrafted surfboard fin featuring tubercle ridges.

BELOW Tubercle-ridge surf fins made from thermoplastic polymers using fibre-deposition additive manufacturing.

BOXFISH

Efficient shape and structure

BIONIC CAR

Aerodynamic lightweight
construction

Boxfish (*Teleostei ostraciidae*) dwell in the shallow waters of tropical reefs. They are, as their name suggests, box-shaped, and unlike most fish, they are rigid creatures, thanks to a bony external structure of thin hexagonal plates that covers most of the body. This exoskeleton protects the animal from impact. The fish moves using a mechanism that involves complex motions of its five fins rather than the body-bending typical of soft-bodied fish. The shape of the animal combined with the rigid structure of its exoskeleton and its powerful fin muscles delivers a unique system that enables movement using minimal amounts of energy.

The spotted boxfish is trapezoidal in shape with a flat back (keel) structure, concave sides and a bumpy texture. This specialized exterior texture enables the fish to passively resist forces of turbulent water by transforming the turbulence into self-stabilizing vortices, a mechanism that allows the fish to move through water in a smooth, energy-efficient trajectory with minimal engagement of fin muscles, thus conserving considerable amounts of energy.

The shape of the boxfish helps it to remain stable in turbulent water.

The Bionic concept car by DaimlerChrysler and Mercedes-Benz, based on aspects of the boxfish.

The carapace, or external skeleton, of the boxfish is made of stiff hexagonal scales fused together.

STREAMLINED CAR

The boxfish uses a combination of simple structural and textural design to deliver strength, stability and agility passively. Scientists at the Mercedes-Benz Technology Centre and DaimlerChrysler Research in Germany combined forces to study these specific aspects of the boxfish and explore opportunities for technology transfer into the automotive sector. There were already obvious similarities between the fish and a car in terms of shape, but in-depth studies of hydro- and aerodynamic properties of the shape and texture, combined with mathematical modelling, revealed that the boxfish, despite its bulky appearance, is in fact highly streamlined. The Mercedes-Benz Bionic concept car was modelled on the boxfish in both shape and structure, resulting in an aerodynamically efficient and lightweight construction.

BIOLOGY

SURFACE

BIOMIMETIC APPLICATION

02

This chapter explores the role of
texture in nature and the way in
which the surface morphology of
a system can introduce a host of
passive properties essential to survival.
Textural qualities such as smooth,
reflective, rough, bumpy and so on play
a significant role in the aesthetics and
ergonomics of design; however, biology
shows us an entirely new perspective
on texture as a platform for advanced
products. This section will demonstrate
why microscopic bumps and lumps are
favoured over flat, smooth surfaces
in biology and how the manipulation
of the scale and design of texture
can be an invaluable tool for resource
optimization and for the introduction
of multifunctional properties into man-
made products.

SHARK SKIN

Drag-reducing properties

SUPERFUNCTIONAL TEXTURE

Antibacterial and anti-adhesion surfaces

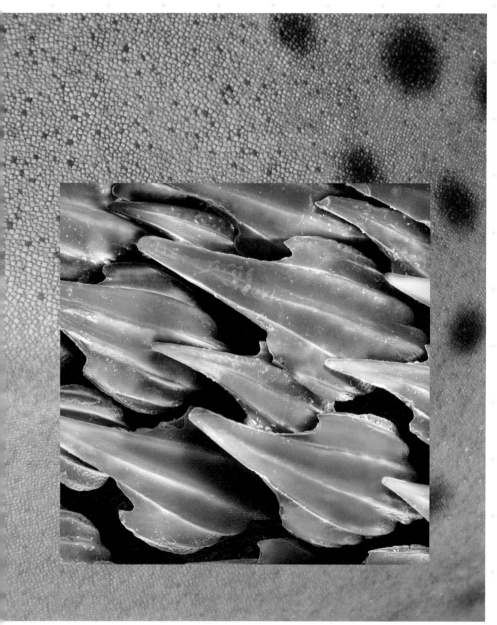

Close-up of shark skin, with (inset) microscopic detail of shark denticles.

Sharks are among the deadliest predators on the planet. The animal's superior stealth, speed and power are attributed to specialized behaviours and tools evolved over millennia. Sharks usually stalk their prey: this means that they spend a great deal of time circling and watching, a relatively low-energy activity. However, they can quickly develop short bursts of speed reaching, in some species, 50 km/h (30 mph) during attack mode, a tactic that startles and catches the prey off guard.

The friction between the surface of an object and the water reduces the speed of flow. Drag is created by the difference between the speed of water flowing over a surface and that of the water flowing away, often causing the formation of vortices that impede trajectory. Like many underwater creatures, sharks are soft-bodied, but they are not covered in scales. Scaly fish have evolved an auxiliary mechanism to reduce this type of drag force: they periodically secrete a slippery substance, or mucus, that covers their bodies. This reduces drag from skin friction and also offers protection from abrasion; additionally, the material prevents microscopic organisms from adhering to the animal's scales (biofouling), thereby protecting from infection, parasites and disease.

Sharks have evolved an incredibly simple yet sophisticated method of managing drag. Instead of scales and mucus, the animals are covered in dermal denticles – microscopic scale-like structures made from skin. Shark denticles, whose size and design varies with species, are tooth-shaped with a ribbed texture of longitudinal grooves aligned with the direction of water flow. The denticles work by channelling the water as it travels over the body. In doing so, they manage the speed and direction of the flow, thus minimizing the size of the vortices created. The resulting drag forces generated by these mini-vortices are so small that they have minimal impact on speed. If the shark's body were smooth and the denticles flat, like fish scales, the difference in water speed would create large turbulent vortices around the animal that would resist motion, thus making it harder for the animal to swim at speed.

A swimmer wearing a full-body swimsuit made from shark denticle mimetic textile.

DRAG REDUCTION IN FLIGHT

Passive drag reduction for air and water vessels is an area of significant interest, as it can improve fuel efficiency. In the summer of 2013, Germany's largest airline, Lufthansa, began a two-year trial to test the properties of shark skin in flight on two of its Airbus A340-300 jets. Eight 10 x 10 centimetre (4 x 4 inch) patches of a new coating were applied to the fuselage and the leading edges of the wings. The novel coating, developed by the Fraunhofer Institute for Manufacturing Technology and Advanced Materials (IFAM) in Bremen, enables the creation of a localized texture on the metal skin that mimics the ribbed structure of shark denticles. A 1 per cent reduction in fuel consumption is estimated for an aircraft covered in between 40 and 70 per cent of the new textured polymer coating – this represents a saving of about 90,000 tonnes of jet fuel per year for Lufthansa.

SWIM FASTER

Imagine if you could put on a swimsuit that could make you swim faster by reducing the drag caused by the friction between your body and the water. Swimwear company Speedo has been exploring drag reduction in swimwear textiles since the late 1980s, and in 2000 it successfully launched FastSkin, a full-body swimsuit made from a biomimetic textile with a texture that imitates shark denticles. During the Sydney 2000 Olympics, athletes in FastSkin swimsuits achieved thirteen out of the fifteen records broken and 83 per cent of medals won. There are, however, many questions within the biomimetic community surrounding the claims made for this technology, as human bodies are very different in shape and structure from sharks and swim in very different ways. It is not clear if it is the surface structure of the textile or the tight-fitting aspect of the suit that enhances performance so greatly (athletes with more body fat saw the most performance enhancement; there was little to no effect on leaner athletes), but during the period 2008–09 when the use of these suits was permitted by FINA (the International Swimming Federation), more than 300 records were set. Today, the use of this type of suit is not permitted in competitive events.

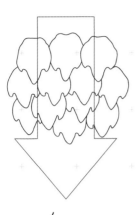

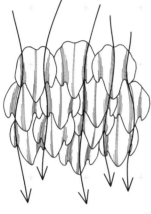

TOP A sheet of water flowing over a flat surface: drag forces created from this configuration are strong.

ABOVE When the water sheet is divided by the microscopic ridges of shark denticles, it is split into much smaller streams, which minimizes the creation of drag forces.

ANTIFOULING TEXTURES

Just like fish mucus, shark dermal denticles also prevent biofouling, though this is due to the structure and shape of the scale, and in particular the distance between the denticles, rather than to the secretion of a polymer. This aspect is of great interest to several sectors, including the medical, aviation and nautical industries. For example, boat hulls require the use of toxic paints, and the frequent removal of vessels from water and resurfacing of hulls. If an antifouling method could be introduced passively through the textured design of hull skin, the reduction in both cost and environmental impact would be significant. Engineered surface textures at microscopic scale have been created to offer passive antimicrobial properties to surfaces simply through the prevention of adhesion.

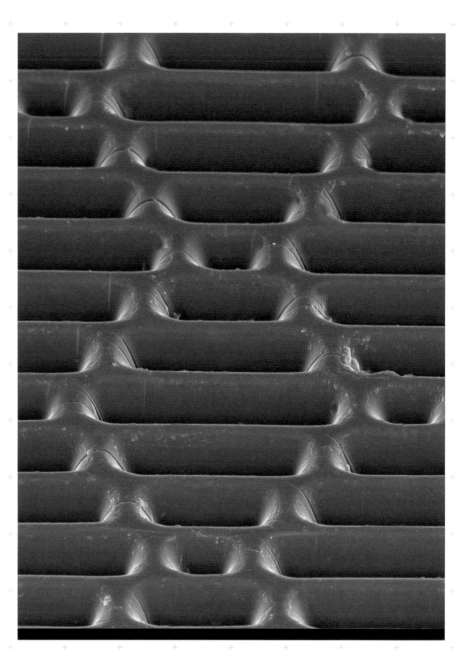

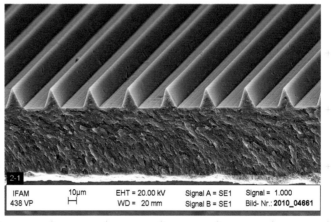

| IFAM | 10µm | EHT = 20.00 kV | Signal A = SE1 | Signal = 1.000 |
| 438 VP | | WD = 20 mm | Signal B = SE1 | Bild- Nr.: 2010_04661 |

ABOVE Zambezi shark.

RIGHT Pressurized water is used to remove biofouling on the stern and propeller of a beached ship.

OPPOSITE TOP A scanning electron micrograph (SEM) of Sharklet, an antibacterial material whose surface structure was inspired by the denticles found on shark skin, which are known to deter bacteria and other microorganisms from establishing a colony. The rough surface requires more energy output from the microorganisms to grow on, which in turn inhibits their growth. The Sharklet film can be applied to frequently touched surfaces such as restroom doors and toilet handles or coated on medical devices and other germ-free equipment.

OPPOSITE BOTTOM Microscopic shark-skin-inspired surface coating for aircraft bodies developed by the Fraunhofer Institute in conjunction with Airbus.

BURDOCK

Hooked seed dispersal mechanism

VELCRO

Reversible hook-and-loop fastening

A burdock seedpod, and (inset) a macro view of the seed needles with their curved tips that resemble hooks.

Plants lack mobility, yet in order to ensure maximum chances of germination (and thus reproduction), most seeds need to travel as far away from the parent plant as possible to avoid competition for water, sunlight and nutrients. As a result, a vast variety of seed dispersal mechanisms has evolved within the plant kingdom. Some seeds rely on the wind, others on being eaten by animals; still others simply hitch a ride. One such example is burdock (genus *Arctium*), a flowering thistle with leaves that can grow up to 70 centimetres (28 inches)

long. Burdock does not produce fruit and most animals avoid consuming it, yet it relies on interaction with animals and humans to disseminate its seeds. It achieves this through clever design: burdock seeds are covered in prickly hairs that attach to animal fur and human clothing and thus are involuntarily carried away from the parent plant.

ABOVE Detail of Velcro application
on a protective garment.

BELOW Close-up detail of hook-
and-loop fastening system.

HOOKS AND LOOPS

In 1941, George de Mestral, a Swiss electrical
engineer and keen mountaineer, wanted to find
out why it was so difficult to remove burrs from
his clothes and his dog's fur after walks in the
mountains. A simple observation of burdock
burrs under the microscope revealed that each
spine ended with a curved tip, resembling a hook.
Mestral spotted the potential for a reversible dry
adhesion system initially for clothing or textile
fasteners, and he began to work with a French

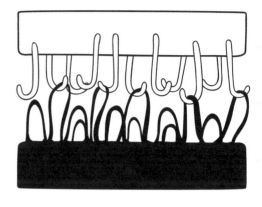

ABOVE LEFT Close-up of Velcro nylon hook-and-loop system.

ABOVE Illustration of hook-and-loop concept. The tiny hooks catch in the loops when the two sides are pressed together, forming a temporary binding of varying degrees of strength.

LEFT Bullet-proof vest with Velcro detail.

textile mill to try to translate his observations into a fibrous hook-and-loop textile fastener.

The first prototypes were made from cotton, but the adhesive properties lasted only a few cycles. Mestral replaced cotton with the newly invented nylon filament, which increased robustness and adhesion repeatability.

Mestral filed for a patent in 1951, which was granted in 1955. The first notable commercial applications were in space suits, followed by skiwear and other active clothing systems. Today Velcro's hook-and-loop system is used in a wide range of applications, from children's shoes to protective clothing.

ABOVE Burdock seedpod.

BELOW Activewear jacket with
Velcro detail.

GECKO FEET

Gravity-defying adhesion

SUPER-ADHESIVE
TEXTURE

Stickiness without glue

A view of a gecko from beneath, with (inset) a close-up of the top of a gecko's foot.

The gecko has puzzled observers and scientists for thousands of years with its gravity-defying ability to effortlessly scale walls and walk across ceilings. Although the mechanism was clearly located in the reptile's feet, it was not until the development of powerful microscopes that the mystery behind this extraordinary behaviour began to unravel. Scientists observed the structure of the gecko's toepad and found a surface covered with about 500,000 microscopic hairs, or setae. The setae are 30–130 microns long (there are 1,000 microns in a millimetre),

while the tip of each fibre is further divided into hundreds of protruding flat spoon-shaped structures (spatulae) ranging from 0.2 to 0.5 microns in diameter.

The first attempts to measure the adhesive forces of the foot of a tokay gecko (*Gekko gecko*) were conducted in the 1990s. The team of scientists leading the study estimated that 6.5 square centimetres (1 square inch) of setae could support 6.6 kilos (14.5 pounds). Roughly speaking, this meant that a million setae, fitting on an American dime, would support the weight

of a small child. A range of hypotheses that could potentially explain the mechanism was considered, but it was not until 2000 that the true mechanism was deduced, when a group of US scientists led by Kellar Autumn from Lewis & Clark College in Portland, Oregon, and Robert Full from the University of California, Berkeley, was able to measure the adhesive force of a single spatula. Using a two-dimensional micro-electro-mechanical sensor, the team found that each spatula could produce about 0.000194 N (newtons) (a medium-sized apple exerts 1 newton of force). Such incredibly weak forces could only be van der Waals – attractive forces that happen at molecular level. With each step, the lizard applies pressure on to its footpad; this engages these weak van der Waals forces between the contacting setae and the surface. Remarkably, the compound effect of the adhesive properties of the total number of setae was calculated to be in the region of 3–20 newtons per square centimetre (5–30 psi), significantly more than needed to support the lizard's own weight.

These findings demonstrated that the mechanism behind the switchable adhesion of the gecko foot – that is, the on/off nature of the stickiness – is a combination of behaviour (the foot pressing down and then the grip being released as the toe curls away from the surface) and the molecular forces of physical attraction created between the setae and the contact surface. The sheer number of setae transforms this weak attraction of nominal strength at individual level into a significant gripping force capable of holding a great deal more than the weight of a small lizard.

ABOVE LEFT Artist's impression of potential gecko technology application: synthetic gecko tips for fingers, enabling individuals to scale a flat surface by sticking to it with their fingertips.

BELOW LEFT Illustration of gecko tape surface microtexture.

ABOVE RIGHT Close-up of gecko toe spatulae.

BELOW RIGHT Illustration of spatulae connecting to a surface by means of van de Waals forces.

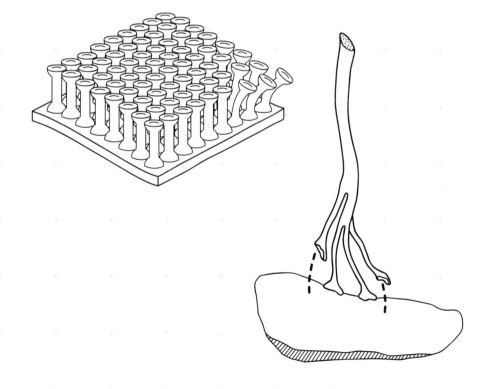

GECKO TAPE

An international team of researchers from the UK's University of Manchester and Russia's Institute for Microelectronic Technology has developed a nanoscale fabrication process that enables it to engineer microscopic hairs on to a tape made from polyimide (a type of strong, lightweight polymer) that demonstrate similar adhesive forces to a single gecko seta. This method is cheaper, quicker and simpler than using electron-beam lithography (a form of 3D printing) and could potentially be upscaled for commercial production. The prototype tape is able to go through several attachment/detachment cycles, but the team is concerned about durability. Further work is under way that explores alternative materials to polyimide, such as keratin (a key component of the gecko setae). The introduction of this type of dry adhesive could have significant impact on the design industry as it offers an invisible alternative to Velcro, whose appearance and aesthetic properties have limited potential applications.

GECKSKIN

Al Crosby and Duncan J. Irschick, professors at the University of Massachusetts Amherst, combined their cross-disciplinary skills and knowledge to develop Geckskin, an alternative way of creating gecko-type adhesion, without the use of nanotechnology. Instead they use a combination of stiff materials such as Kevlar or carbon fibre with soft elastomers such as polyurethane or polydimethylsiloxane (PDMS).

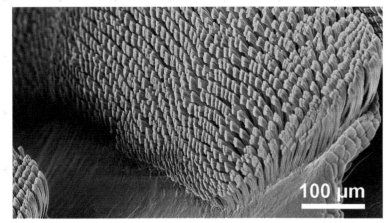

TOP Examples of Geckskin fabric.

ABOVE Close-up of gecko setae.

RIGHT The gecko 'switches off' the adhesive properties of its footpad by curling its toes away from the contacting surface.

ABOVE View of the setae forming rows of lamellae, or ridges, that line the toes of the gecko.

LEFT Geckskin fabrics in application – holding very heavy objects without glue.

BELOW Close-up of gecko setae.

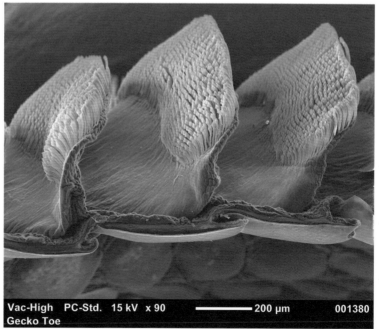

Vac-High   PC-Std.   15 kV   x 90   ———— 200 µm   001380
Gecko Toe

LOTUS LEAF
Self-cleaning superhydrophobic properties

BIOMIMETIC APPLICATION
LOTUS EFFECT
Self-cleaning surfaces

I love the lotus because, while growing from mud, it is unstained.

Zhou Dunyi (1017–1073)
Chinese Neo-Confucian philosopher

Water droplets on the
surface of a lotus leaf.

Scanning electron micrograph (SEM) of the surface of a lotus leaf. The top of the leaf contains microstructures that repel water droplets better than any other material in nature.

The lotus plant (*Nelumbo nucifera*) holds a sacred place in many Eastern cultures. It is a symbol of purity, non-attachment and divine beauty, characteristics attributed to the plant partly because of its remarkable ability to remain clean despite its muddy habitat. The mechanism behind this extraordinary behaviour remained a mystery until the early 1970s and the invention of the scanning electron microscope (SEM). A team led by German botanist and bionics expert Wilhelm Barthlott studied the surface structure of lotus leaves using the SEM, and discovered that the epidermis, or cuticle, of the lotus leaf is rough. The cuticle surface is covered with microscopic bumps, or papillae, about 10–20 microns high and 10–15 microns wide, and each of these papillae is itself topped with an epicuticular wax crystalloid – a waxy structure that resembles a cone with a rounded tip, 1–5 microns in height.

Although the epicuticular wax is naturally hydrophobic, or water-repellent, it is the positioning of the papillae and wax structures that is responsible for the superhydrophobic self-cleaning function. First, the specialized design of the texture combines with air to create a composite low-energy surface that prevents water drops from spreading – instead, spherical droplets are formed, which roll along the surface of the leaf. Second, the distance between the wax crystalloids is smaller than the surface of dirt particles, pathogens or other contaminants, meaning that foreign particles sit on the tips of the wax crystalloids and away from the surface of the leaf, keeping the contact area to a minimum. As a water droplet rolls along the surface of the leaf, it picks up the particles and carries them away, thereby cleaning the surface. Barthlott and his team coined the term 'lotus effect' to describe this property.

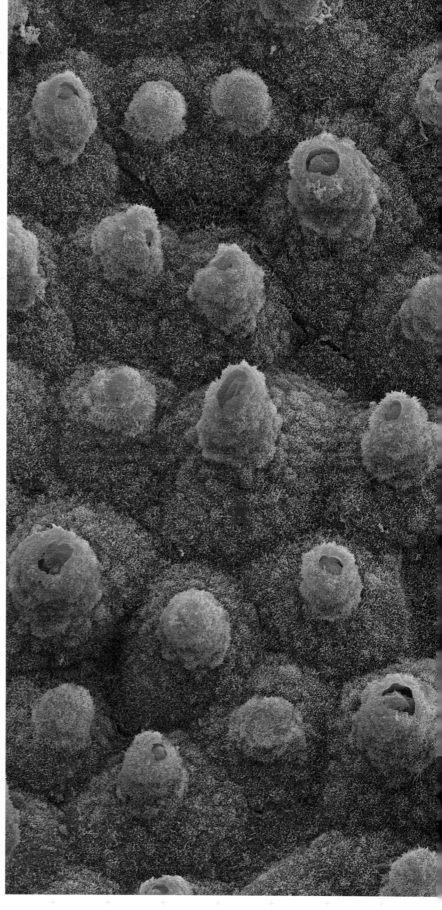

SELF-CLEANING PAINT AND TEXTILES

The first industrial application for the lotus effect was in the form of a self-cleaning masonry paint called Lotusan. The paint creates a surface microstructure that resembles the wax-tipped papillae of the lotus leaf in both form and scale. Façades coated in Lotusan recreate the superhydrophobic properties of the lotus leaf to allow passive self-cleaning during rainfall, thus requiring significantly less maintenance.

There are numerous opportunities for passive-cleaning, soil-repellent technologies in the textile industry. Currently, coatings such as Teflon are applied to textiles with compounds made from silicone or organofluorochemicals to deliver superhydrophobic self-cleaning properties, but this is a process that requires both high energy consumption and toxic materials. A true lotus effect can be achieved by engineering the surface of a textile using plasma treatment, a low-energy process that does not involve the use of harsh chemicals, but is currently more expensive.

LEFT ABOVE Illustration of leaf surface microstructure with water droplets and dirt particles.

LEFT CENTRE Water droplets on a Lotusan-coated wall surface, showing the self-cleaning effect.

LEFT Water droplet on lotus leaf surface.

OPPOSITE Water droplets on a shirt treated with lotus-type finish.

BIOLOGY

MORPHO BUTTERFLY

Structural coloration

BIOMIMETIC APPLICATION

MORPHOTEX

Pigment-less coloured textiles

Humans perceive colour through the interaction of the light spectrum with the light receptors in the eye. The most common mechanism used to generate colour in both biology and technology is through pigments. Pigments are small particles of material that alter the colour of transmitted light by absorbing specific wavelengths. Originally we extracted pigments from natural sources such as plants and minerals and mixed them with liquids or into pastes to create paints, dyes and so on. More recently, advances in chemistry have delivered a large portfolio of artificial counterparts compatible with new synthetic materials. The use of colour is essential in the creative industries and is firmly embedded in culture and society: evidence of humans using pigment to introduce colour to textiles dates back more than 5,000 years. Today, however, the industrial colouring of textiles and other man-made products is a highly toxic and unsustainable practice.

An alternative method of creating colour, common among animals and insects, is known as structural coloration, by which colour is created by a variety of photonic (light) mechanisms. Such colours are known as schemochromes. Rather than by means of tiny light-absorbing particles, colour is generated by the way in which the microstructure of a scale, feather or shell interferes with reflected light. The South American morpho butterfly has characteristic brilliant blue wings whose colour is attributed exclusively to surface structure rather than pigment. Morpho butterfly wings are covered in tiny scales of chitin (a fibrous substance), whose micro-surface resembles rows of trees; this array creates a surface texture that reflects light and disperses it in different directions. The distance between the chitin rows determines the iridescent blue colour.

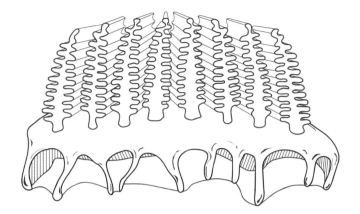

OPPOSITE Abstract blue texture of a shiny morpho
butterfly wing, with (inset) the morpho butterfly.

LEFT Illustration of the microstructure covering
the surface of morpho butterfly wing scales.

BELOW Close-up detail of butterfly wing scales.

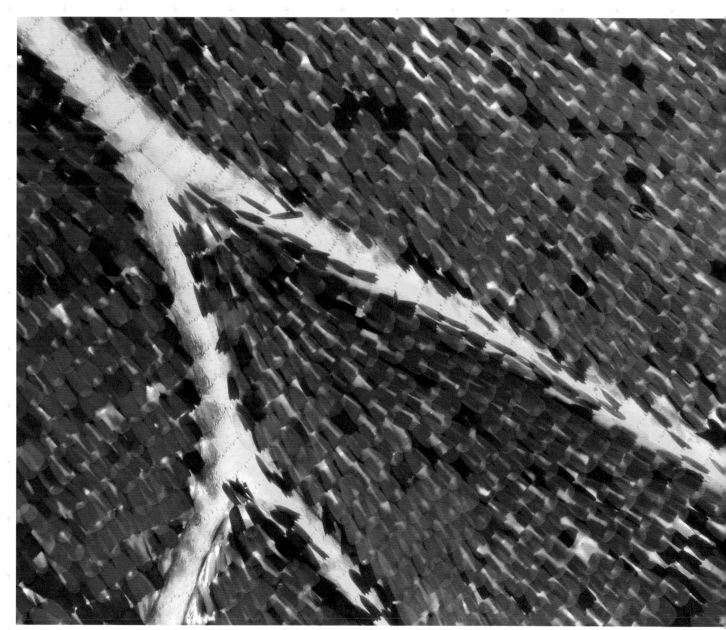

STRUCTURAL-COLOURED
TEXTILES

Morphotex, developed by the Japanese company
Teijin Fibers Limited, is the first commercial
fibre technology that uses structure rather than
pigment and dyes to introduce colour. Inspired
by the surface structure of the morpho butterfly
wing, researchers at Teijin designed a fibre made
of sixty-one alternating nylon and polyester layers
that imitate the tree-row surface of the morpho
wing, and which is capable of producing basic
colours such as blue, green and red without the
use of pigments simply by altering the distance
between the ridges. This technology offers an
alternative, less hazardous method of introducing
colour to textiles.

Donna Sgro, a practice-led researcher and
fashion designer based in Sydney, created
the first structural-coloured garment using
Morphotex for Japan's Shinmai Creator's project
in 2009. Unfortunately, Morphotex fibres are not
commercially available currently because low
market demand prevents the production
of sustainable volumes.

RIGHT Dress made from Morphotex
fabric by Donna Sgro.

BELOW Paint pigments on display in
the sun in Kathmandu, Nepal.

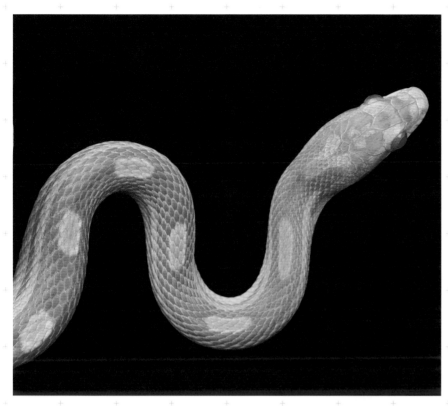

LEFT Colourful skin pigmentation of the motley corn snake.

BELOW Pigmentation in close-up detail of an orchid flower.

STARFISH
PEDICELLARIAE

Active self-cleaning and defensive surface

MICRO-GRIPPING
TEXTURE

Advanced smart surfaces

Starfish have a tough outer skin made of plates of calcium carbonate covered in tiny spines that serve to protect them from predators.

ABOVE Orange starfish arm detail.

BELOW Illustration of starfish pedicellaria open and closing mechanism.

Echinoderms such as sea urchins and starfish have bodies covered in tiny claw-shaped structures, known as pedicellariae, that keep the organism's surface clear of algae and other encrusting organisms and act as a deterrent to pests and predators. The tiny claws sense the presence of a threatening object and respond by clenching tightly, capturing or gripping it.

The echinoderm pedicellaria structure consists of a jaw made up of three tooth-like structures located at the top of a shaft. A specialized muscle enclosed within the shaft controls the opening and closing of the jaw, which when closed usually forms a hollow cavity, depending on species. These structures range from 250 to 500 microns in width and from 500 to 1000 microns in height.

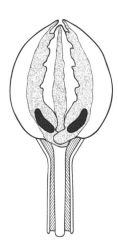
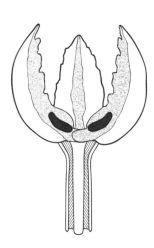

ACTIVE GRIPPING SURFACE

Scientists from the British universities of Warwick and Birmingham collaborated to replicate this mechanism to create an active gripping surface, using specialist flexible resins and micro-stereolithography – an advanced additive manufacturing technique based on 3D stereolithography that enables the production of very complex 3D structures at micro scale.

The design for the active surface, based on the pedicellaria structure, features sets of jaws with four teeth projecting from the surface of a membrane suspended above a chamber, which can be flooded with air or water to control the opening and closing of the jaws. The system is also designed to have a responsive mode of operation where the jaws are closed or activated when pressure is applied at the centre of the open jaw. The team has identified numerous medical applications for this type of active gripping surface, such as low-cost disposable devices, microrobotics for healthcare and process automation, and functional surfaces for domestic products.

LEFT Artist's impression of micro-gripping surface.

BELOW Starfish detail.

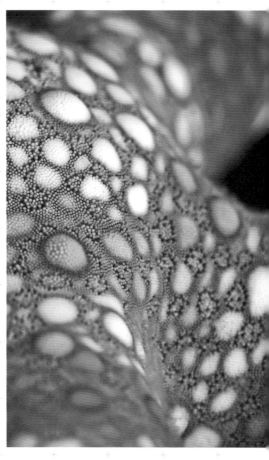

b)

c)

Prototype active gripping surface created by scientists at Warwick and Birmingham universities, made from specialist flexible resins using micro-stereolithography.

LEAF STOMATA | STOMATEX

Plant respiration | Breathable technical textiles

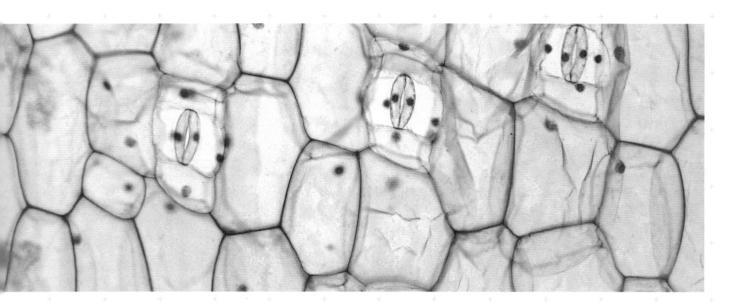

Plants breathe through microscopic pores in the epidermal surface of leaves known as stomata. These pores are mostly found on the underside of leaves and play a critical role in the life and survival of plants. Stomata manage the exchange of gases (carbon dioxide, oxygen and moisture vapour) between the plant and the environment by opening and closing like microscopic mouths. When open, carbon dioxide, a vital component for photosynthesis, diffuses into the leaf from the environment, and at the same time water vapour is lost from the leaf to the surrounding air in a process known as transpiration.

There are many things we still do not know about the stoma mechanism; however, we do know that the pores usually open in the light and close in the dark, with the exception of some desert plants. They tend to open when there are low concentrations of carbon dioxide inside the leaf and close in high concentrations, and can be influenced by many environmental factors, including temperature, humidity, light, and the presence of gaseous pollutants such as sulphur dioxide and ozone.

The opening and closing of each stoma is controlled by two guard cells, which are specialized epidermal cells surrounding each pore. Changes in the internal pressure of these guard cells affect the degree of stoma opening; high internal pressure causes the guard cells to swell and the stoma to increase in size, creating an open pore, while low internal pressure causes the guard cells to shrink and the stoma to close.

ABOVE A microscopic view of the leaf surface of spiderwort, showing stomata.

BELOW Illustration of the Stomatex textile structure, in which the principles of stomata gas exchange are applied to performance clothing.

OPPOSITE Micrograph of a green leaf showing stomata.

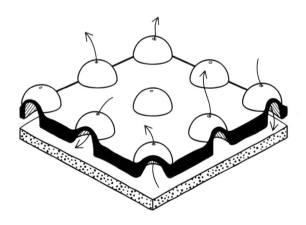

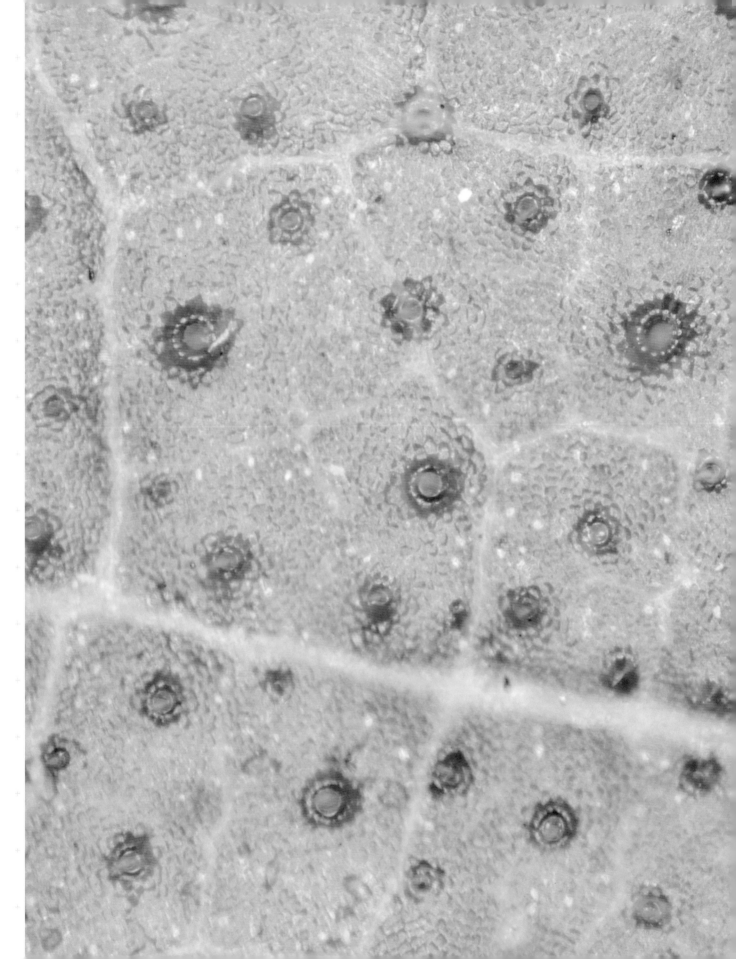

ABOVE Magnified view of rice stomata.

RIGHT Artist's impression of Stomatex application in active clothing.

OPPOSITE Close-up detail of Stomatex fabric, showing the tiny dome-shaped chambers that replicate the function of a plant's stomata.

TRANSPIRATIONAL TEXTILES

The transpirational function of stomata inspired the development of Stomatex textiles for applications in tight-fitting next-to-skin apparel. Stomatex is made from neoprene, a high-performance composite fabric typically used in scuba-diving suits.

Stomatex fabrics are designed to apply the principles of stomata gas exchange to performance apparel for the management of microclimate conditions between the skin and fabric. The water vapour exchange demonstrated by the stoma pore is recreated in the textile by the introduction of a unique pattern of dome-shaped chambers, each with a tiny hole in the centre. Excess body heat and perspiration rise into the chambers and are released through the hole as the chambers flex and stretch during body movement. This allows the warm, damp air to exit the wearer's microclimate in a controlled way and cooler, drier air to enter from the outside. Current applications include heat acclimatization suits used by athletes preparing for competitions in hot, humid climates; and orthopaedic supports.

THORNY DEVIL

Skin hydraulics

PASSIVE WATER HARVESTING AND DISTRIBUTION

Dynamic hydraulic surfaces

ABOVE Illustration of thorny devil mechanisms for passive water distribution.

LEFT AND OPPOSITE Thorny devil.

The thorny devil lizard (*Moloch horridus*) dwells in the extremely harsh, dry terrain of the central Australian desert and has evolved to survive on a diet consisting mainly of ants. The secret to the lizard's survival is its characteristic 'thorny' skin surface: it is covered in elongated, pointed scales that resemble spikes or thorns. Although the scales function as an effective defence mechanism against predators, the skin structure serves another extraordinary function. Its design allows the animal to passively extract all the water it needs directly from rain, dew, small puddles of water or soil moisture, defying gravity without a pumping device. On the surface of the lizard's skin is a circulatory system made from semi-enclosed channels 5–150 microns wide that run between the spiky scales. These channels draw the moisture through them and distribute it to the lizard's mouth using capillary forces.

WATER MANAGEMENT

The potential for passive collection and distribution of water is significant. It could help provide clean water supplies to the billion people who live in extreme conditions, whether in times of drought or consistently lacking a safe water supply. Buildings could manage water flow without the need for pumps, thus reducing energy consumption and managing building internal temperature through evaporative cooling rather than conventional energy-rich air-conditioning systems.

The Namib beetle fog basking in the
Namib Desert.

By 2025 half of the world's population will be living in water-stressed areas.

World Health Organization, 2015

The Namib Desert is one of the hottest and most arid places on the planet; situated on the southwest coast of Africa, it receives less than 1.5 centimetres (0.6 inches) of rain per year. This hostile environment is home to one of the world's most remarkable insects, the Namib beetle (*Stenocara gracilipes*) – a creature that manages to drink in an environment devoid of any form of running water.

The Namib beetle is able to defy the nature of its habitat thanks to a combination of behavioural and design factors. Its hardened forewing shell has a specialized microscopic bumpy texture comprising hydrophilic (water-attracting) peaks, approximately 100–500 microns in diameter, and valleys covered in a

Fog-harvesting net featuring both
hydrophobic and hydrophilic surfaces.

waxy material that renders them hydrophobic
(water-repelling), approximately 500–1,500
microns wide. Under the waxy coating the
valleys are lined with a hexagonal pattern of tiny
hemispheres, and together the hydrophobic
materials and the hexagonal substructure create
a superhydrophobic pathway.

In the presence of the thick fog that frequently
rolls in off the South Atlantic during the night
and early mornings, the Namib beetles face into
the wind and raise their rear ends into the air, a
behaviour dubbed 'fog basking'. Fog is made of
tiny moisture microdroplets about 1–40 microns
in diameter that float in the air: these droplets
attach themselves to the hydrophilic peaks of the
beetle shell and grow in size as more and more

microdroplets combine to form a drop. Once the
drop reaches 4–5 millimetres (approx. 0.2 inch)
in diameter, it trickles down to the hydrophobic
valleys, which direct the water to the beetle's
mouth.

FOG HARVESTING

Fog harvesting offers a promising method of
achieving a clean, safe water supply. Devices
for extracting clean water from fog date back to
the 1990s – large panels of net fabric stretched
across a fence-like frame are used to catch the
fog droplets, which drip into repositories – but
these fog-catching nets are not efficient enough
to deliver meaningful volumes of water.

Shreerang Chhatre, a chemical engineer from
the Massachusetts Institute of Technology (MIT),
combined his knowledge of the wettability of
materials (their tendency to either absorb or
repel liquids) with studies on *Stenocara gracilipes*
to try to improve the yield of conventional fog-
harvest devices. Chhatre realized that in order
to transfer the Namib beetle functionality the
new harvesting system must have a combination
of surfaces that attract and repel water just
like the shell's microtexture. Chhatre and his
team developed synthetic surfaces mimicking
the beetle's back that are several times more
effective than their predecessors, with potential
applications in arid regions and refugee camps
and even on the tops of skyscrapers.

OPPOSITE Concept image of a self-filling water bottle.

BOTTOM The O2 Arena in London offers a large potential surface for a water-harvesting mechanism.

BELOW Illustration of Namib beetle shell texture including hydrophilic and hydrophobic areas.

SELF-FILLING WATER BOTTLES

NBD Nano was set up by a duo of Boston College graduates hoping to mimic the Namib beetle shell to create the world's first self-filling water bottles. Co-founders Deckard Sorenson and Miguel Galvez enlisted the help of Andy McTeague, a chemist from MIT, to recreate the materials on the shell surface. McTeague created a material using nanotechnology to optimize the collection of condensation; the team believes that this technology could harvest 3 litres per square metre (150 cubic inches per yard) per hour in an area with 75 per cent humidity.

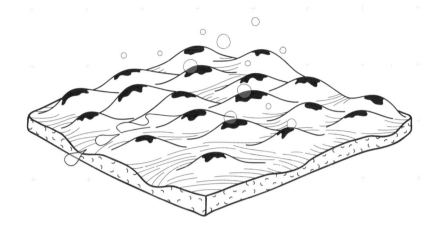

03

STRUCTURE

BIOMIMETIC APPLICATION

OPPOSITE TOP Detail of a skyscraper framework: beams made from structural steel are bolted together at right angles to each other. This is a single-order hierarchical structure.

OPPOSITE BOTTOM Detail of the Eiffel Tower structure: iron beams are bolted together forming a latticework tower. This is a third-order hierarchical structure.

This chapter delves deeper into the role of materials in the context of biomimetic principles to reveal further opportunities for design. Materials in nature are limited: there are essentially two main polymer groups – proteins and polysaccharides – which form the building blocks of all biological systems and deliver the multitude of properties and functions necessary to sustain life. An ingenious approach to design in biology has emerged to compensate for the restriction on raw material variety: the complex, multifunctional nature of biological systems is mainly due to structural hierarchy (solids composed of structural elements that are themselves composed of smaller structural elements and so on), in which material is assembled, rather than to properties arising from chemistry.

By contrast, we rely on the inherent properties of a material to introduce strength, elasticity and so on to a product. If we need to improve the strength of a bridge, we make stronger steel or use more material; we do not use the same material and review the design. Today, there are more than 300 types of commercial polymers used to manufacture our products, many of which derive from increasingly depleted natural resources, require vast amounts of energy and toxic processes to produce, and end up in landfill.

In 1993, Roderick Lakes from the University of Wisconsin conducted a pivotal study on structural hierarchy in man-made structures. In the study, Lakes compared the Eiffel Tower, an example of hierarchical design, with the non-hierarchical (also known as single-order hierarchical) design of a conventional skyscraper. The latticework tower is composed of 18,000 pieces joined together using bolts and rivets: smaller crossbeams bolted on to larger crossbeams combine to create the tower, revealing three orders of hierarchy. Conventional skyscraper frameworks, conversely, are single-order designs in which beams are bolted together at right angles to each other. The Eiffel Tower is made from iron, a material significantly weaker than modern structural steel; when it was constructed in 1889, critics claimed that the material used was too weak to support the weight of the structure and that the tower would eventually collapse. Yet comparing the relative density of both buildings, Lake found that the Eiffel Tower could support its own weight using about five times less material of inferior strength when compared to a less complex design using stronger material.

Nature shows us how advanced, complex behaviours can emerge from a hierarchical approach to design.

GIANT REED STEM

Strong structures of minimal material

TECHNICAL STEM

Superstrong braided beams

A farm hand harvesting mature giant reeds, with (inset) giant reed cane drying on a cane plantation, France.

Giant reed (*Arundo donax*) stems can grow to 6 metres (20 feet) tall but are only 2 centimetres (0.8 inch) wide. The stem is hollow and made out of cellulose and lignin. With an aspect ratio (ratio of width to height) of 1:300, these remarkable structures are light and strong, and able to withstand strong structural loads (for example, wind). The giant reed draws on minimal amounts of material to create an extremely strong yet lightweight superstructure. Another plant that has similar characteristics is the horsetail (*Equisetum hyemale*).

In 2006 a team of biomimetic scientists led by Markus Milwich at the Institute of Textile Technology and Process Engineering (ITV) in Denkendorf, southern Germany, identified the structures of both horsetail and giant reed stems as effective paradigms for the development of a lightweight beam with high bend resistance, and envisioned applications in the building and architectural sectors.

Hollow beams are a known principle in engineering. Bending resistance is maximized when the majority of the material is located as far away from the centre as possible; however, we tend to rely on the inherent strength of the material (steel) for beam strength. Steel is a finite resource that requires immense energy

to process (temperature and pressure) and is not always produced locally.

Anatomical studies and functional analysis conducted by the team at ITV on horsetail stems revealed that their remarkable properties derive from the way the cellulose and lignin are arranged within the skin. Observations of the stem cross-section reveal an outer skin of tissue made from tightly packed cellulose microfibrils (strands) oriented in parallel to the length of the stem and strengthened with lignin. This outer skin is lined with a series of narrower tubes made of similar material, whose cellulose microfibrils are wound round the tubes in a helix (spiral). These are connected to the skin with a flexible spongy tissue made mostly of less-oriented cellulose.

RIGHT Light photomicrograph of a bamboo stem cross-section viewed through a microscope.

BELOW Illustration of technical plant stem design.

BOTTOM LEFT Image of technical plant stem produced using advanced braiding technologies.

BOTTOM RIGHT Detail of a commercial braiding machine.

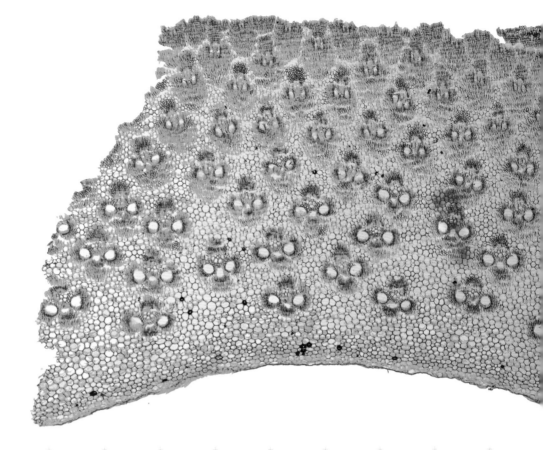

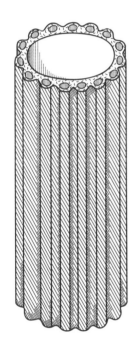

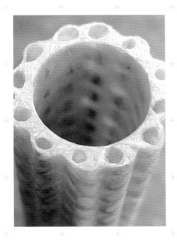

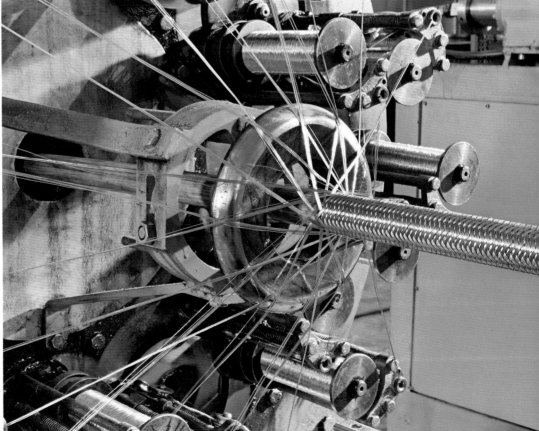

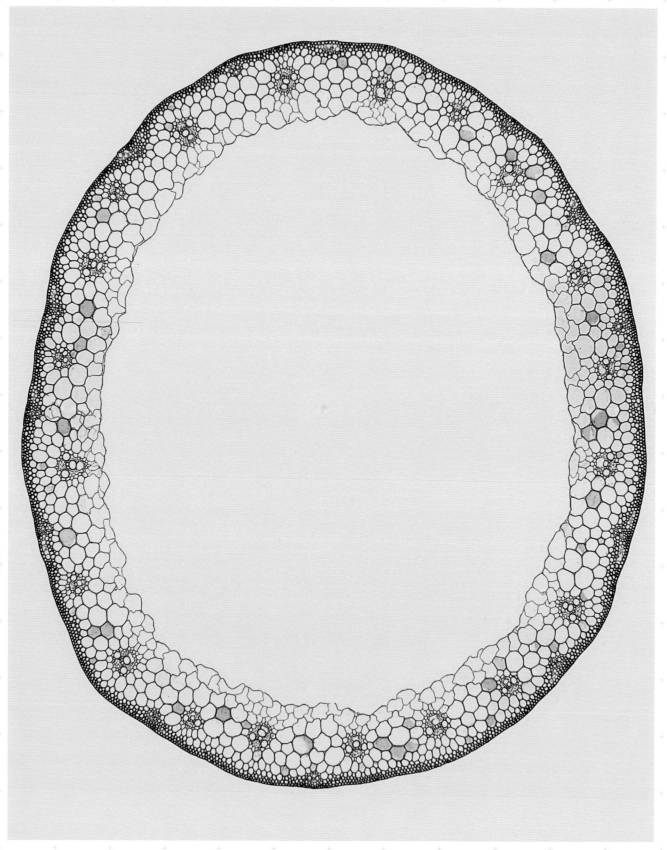

OPPOSITE Cross-section of a young wheat stem, magnification 40x.

RIGHT Light photomicrograph of a cotton stem cross-section viewed through a microscope.

LIGHTWEIGHT STRUCTURAL TUBES

Milwich and his team employed an advanced textile braid-pultrusion system to create a composite textile tube system based on the design ideas that emerged from the botanical observations. Pultrusion is a continuous moulding process resulting in parts with a constant cross-section. Textile braiding is an ancient technique with modern applications and is used in this project to introduce fibre bundles at varying angles to the axis of the tubes. The state-of-the-art equipment used at ITV enables accurate control of the density and angle of the fibres. Two counter-rotating sets of fibre are woven into a helical structure around an inner layer of unidirectional fibres to create tubes, which are later impregnated with a thermoset resin.

These biomimetic textile tubes present a way of creating stiff, strong yet very lightweight structures that could replace metal beams in architecture, but also present a promising framework for the development of strong woven skins for buildings or for aeroplanes and other vehicles.

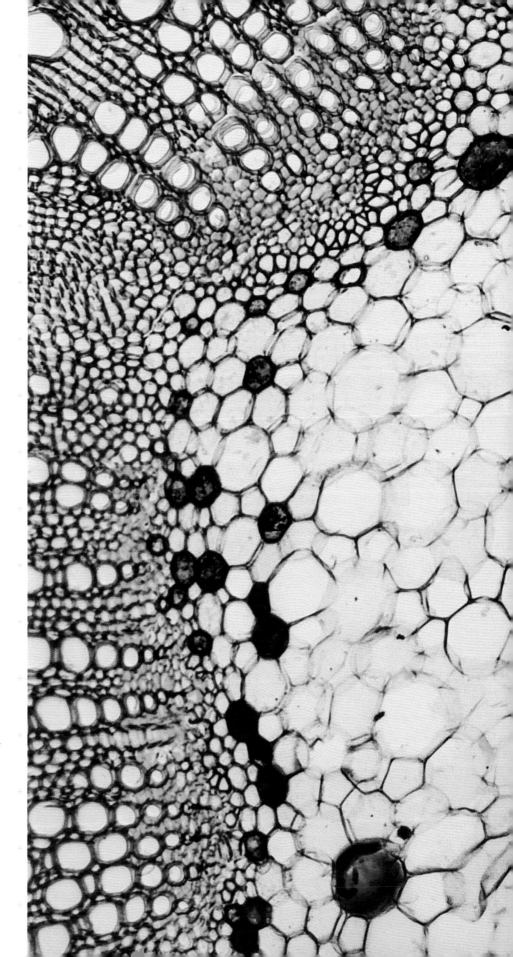

HONEYCOMB

Multifunctional homes of weak material

AIRLESS TYRES

Sustainable puncture-resistant wheels

Solid structures in nature are rare; low-density cellular assemblies such as wood and bone are more common, requiring significantly less material and also delivering unique properties thanks to their structural design. Made from hundreds of hexagonal units, honeybee combs are one of the largest examples of cellular structures in nature. Each cell is about 6 millimetres (0.24 inch) wide and designed to have multiple roles.

The basic building material is wax, secreted from the bodies of worker bees. Beeswax is a weak material whose mechanical integrity diminishes as temperature increases (it becomes softer), yet the combs become stronger and more resilient as they age. The cells themselves are multifunctional containers that offer storage for honey as well as protection and shelter to honeybee larvae during pupation. Once the larvae are sealed in the cells they coat the interior with a layer of randomly oriented silk fibres. Each generation of larvae adds a layer of silk that becomes embedded in the wax. This transforms the structure into a silk/wax composite, which improves its mechanical performance at higher temperatures. This clever yet simple design enables the creation of a strong, multifunctional structure using the minimum amount of material.

ABOVE LEFT A bee at work on a beehive.

ABOVE A section of honeycomb showing the characteristic cellular structure.

OPPOSITE Close-up of man-made sponge made from cellulose.

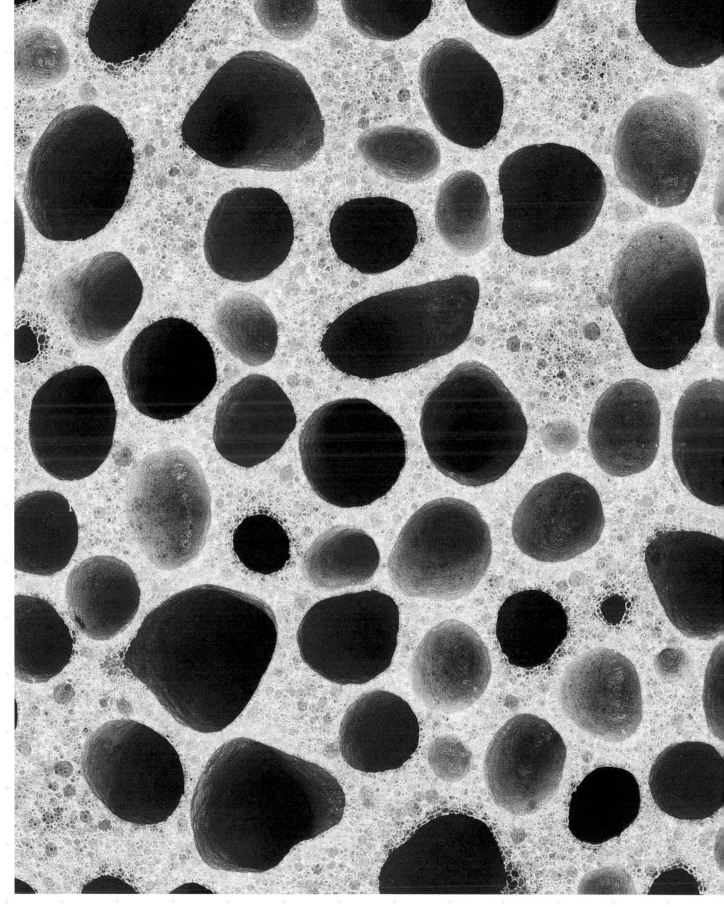

ABOVE Michelin Tweel airless tyres.

RIGHT Hankook Tire's iFlex airless tyres.

CELLULAR TYRES

This type of cellular structure inspired the design
of a new class of wheel. Automobile wheels
are usually made from a steel core that offers
strong, load-bearing capability and fitted with a
pneumatic tyre that delivers shock absorption
during surface contact. However, once punctured
the tyre loses pressure and reduces the vehicle's
mobility. Despite reuse and recycling efforts,
a vast proportion of scrap tyres ends up in
landfill every year. The cellular design of the
non-pneumatic tyre, as its name suggests, does
not rely on air for impact absorption; instead, the
structure takes on that role, enabling the vehicle
to retain mobility following numerous punctures
or damage, significantly extending the useful life
of the product and, since it requires no inner tube,
reducing the number of materials used in the
system so that it is easier to repair or recycle.

Bridgestone airless concept tyre.

Detail of Dunlop tennis racket
biomimetic surface texture.

DUNLOP BIOMIMETIC TENNIS RACKET

Dunlop has developed a novel series of specialist rackets for tennis and squash that combine three biomimetic technologies designed to enhance athletic performance. First, the racket structure features a cellular hexagonal honeycomb system, branded HM6 Carbon, which is made from a specialized carbon compound and, thanks to the cellular design, reduces the racket weight by using less material.

Second, the racket head rim is lined with a tiny ribbed texture based on shark denticles (see p.50). This design feature, branded Aeroskin, is estimated to reduce aerodynamic drag by up to 25 per cent, thus increasing the racket speed and power.

Finally, a tape featuring a specialized microtexture, branded Gecko-Tac, lines the handle; this novel tape is designed to apply a gecko-type texture (see p.58) that creates a type of temporary adhesion between the racket and the skin of the athlete's hand. Dunlop claims that this innovative surface improves grip by 50 per cent as compared to previous gripping systems (although the functionality of this particular application can be obstructed by the use of grip liners preferred by experienced tennis players to protect the racket handle).

TOP The Aeroskin texture on the frame improves the aerodynamic performance of the racket.

ABOVE Detail of Dunlop tennis racket gecko-type grip.

NATURAL CELLULAR SYSTEMS

Minimal-material stiff structures

MINIMAL-MATERIAL PRODUCTS

Ultra-lightweight cellular furniture

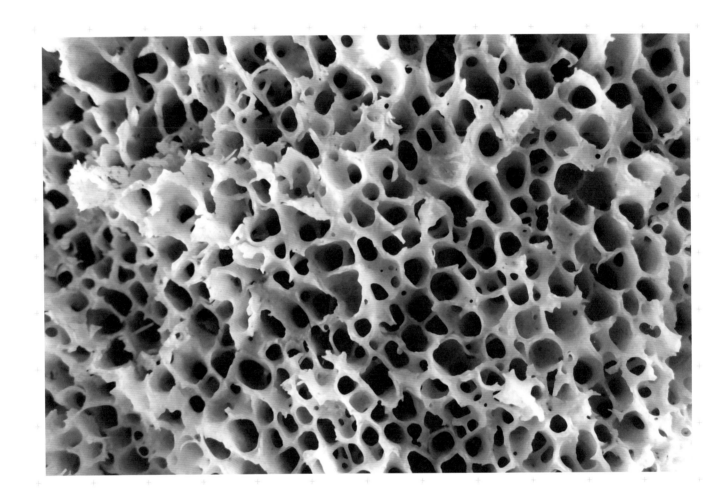

Strong materials such as metals, reinforced plastics and super-tough polymers are essential components in our modern built environments. We rely on the strength of these materials to keep things up, but nature shows us that we can make strong structures from weak materials.

CELLULAR FURNITURE

Koji Sekita is a visionary designer who graduated from Tokyo's prestigious Kuwasawa Design School in 1996 and went on to work as an interior

and furniture designer for firms such as Idee Co. Ltd and Kubota Architects & Associates Inc., before setting up Sekita Design Studio in 2011. Sekita is an agile thinker able to navigate creative and engineering design spaces seamlessly; his work 'Wall of refraction' demonstrates his ability to manipulate light as if it were a piece of paper.

Sekita's signature collection, 'Watching You', is a furniture system made simply of a few sheets of paper shaped through scoring, cutting and folding. This work embraces the biomimetic principle of maximizing resources

and demonstrates how a strong structure can emerge from weak materials. Each sheet of cardstock is scored and folded into identical zigzag structures. Slotting one individual structure into another to form a chair, table or bench creates a hierarchical system. The modular nature of the assembly process enables the creation of products of any length. Sekita's biomimetic approach to design enables the creation of logic-defying, strong yet ultra-lightweight functional furniture from simple materials with little energy input.

OPPOSITE Detail view of trabecular, or spongy, bone tissue. The structure is composed of a stiff microscopic tissue that resembles criss-crossing beams positioned along the lines of mechanical load. Koji Sekita applies this porous cellular design principle to the creation of furniture made from folded and cut pieces of cardboard. The direction of the cardboard structure is aligned with the mechanical loads applied to the furniture during use.

RIGHT Koji Sekita cellular furniture collection made from paper, with (centre) the 'Watching You' modular chair and (bottom) the 'I'll Be There' table.

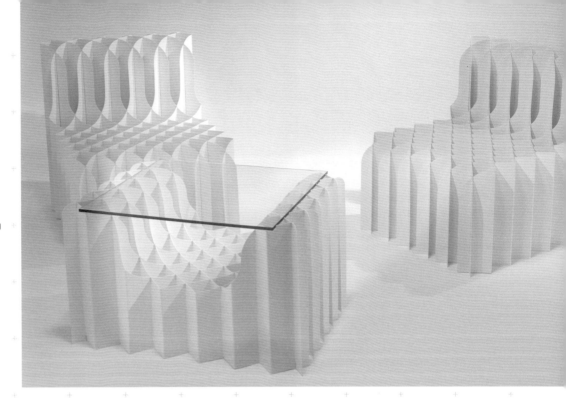

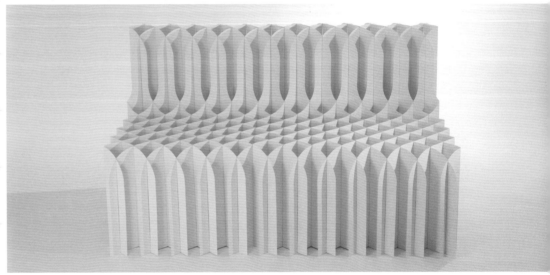

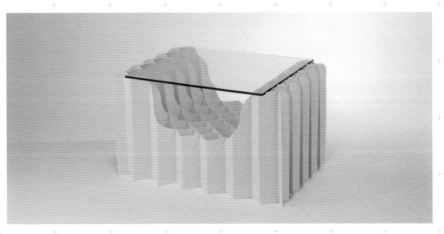

BIOLOGY

NATURAL CELLULAR
STRUCTURES

Stiffness by design

BIOMIMETIC APPLICATION

SINGLE-MATERIAL
PRODUCTS

3D-printed furniture

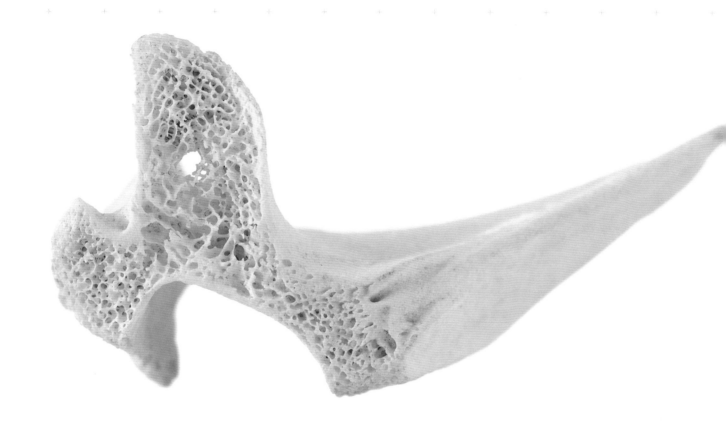

Lilian van Daal's 3D-printed chair (detail, left) makes use of the combination of spongy qualities and stiff structural properties of bone tissue (above).

Our dependence on material properties for functionality results in multimaterial products that, among other things, discourage disassembly, recycling and decomposition. For example, soft furniture, such as sofas and armchairs, requires a variety of materials for its construction, including soft and hard components. Could biology suggest ways of creating furniture from a single material that could be soft and hard by design?

BELOW Side view of Lilian van Daal's
3D-printed chair.

BOTTOM Detail of the cellular design
of Lilian van Daal's chair.

MONO-MATERIAL CELLULAR FURNITURE DESIGN

In 2014, as her graduation project on the postgraduate course in industrial design at the Royal College of Art in The Hague, Lilian van Daal set out to address this issue and develop an alternative approach to the production of soft furniture. Inspired by biological cellular systems such as bone, van Daal identified 3D printing as a key enabling technology that would allow her to engineer furniture from a single material yet be able to introduce local soft and hard regions by manipulating material density through design. This pioneering approach offers a promising alternative to furniture production that circumnavigates the intense processing and logistics and the resulting energy and resource consumption of current industrial practice. Van Daal collaborated with 3D Systems Benelux to produce her prototype chair design.

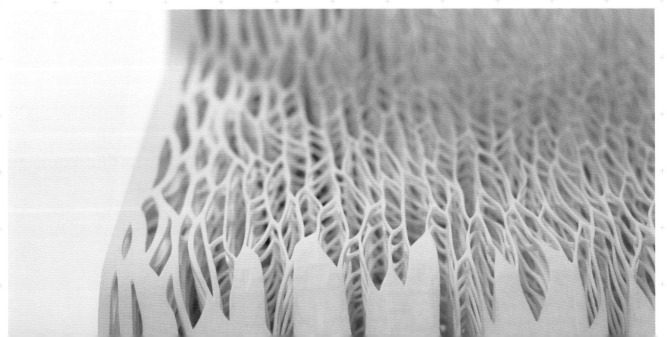

AUXETIC
MATERIALS

Negative Poisson's ratio

BLAST-RESISTANT
TEXTILES

Auxetic yarns and foams

Cellular biological materials demonstrate a host of extraordinary properties due to the geometry of the cell structure. Generally, materials become fatter when compressed and thinner when stretched. The ratio of transverse contraction to longitudinal extension is called the Poisson's ratio. Most materials have a Poisson's ratio of between 0 and 0.5; strong engineering materials have a Poisson's ratio of around 0.3 (steel 0.27–0.3, aluminium 0.32, titanium 0.33), while rubber has a value of around 0.5. Certain biological materials, including cork, bone and various skins, have been found to have a value of 0, or even negative in some cases.

Cork is a low-density cellular material formed of bark harvested from the cork oak (*Quercus suber*), most commonly used to make wine bottle stoppers. Cork cells are so small that 20,000 could fit into a cubic millimetre. Generally they have a hexagonal cross-section, but the cell walls exhibit an extraordinary corrugated structure that allows them to extend and become flat when pulled and fold like a concertina when compressed. This specialized microscopic cell design delivers a unique material system with a Poisson's ratio of 0 that enables cork to be used as a mechanical glass bottle seal, since it does not expand in width when compressed.

Structures exhibiting a negative Poisson's ratio were first observed in the 1940s, during the study of iron pyrite crystals. Although the phenomenon was initially dismissed as an anomaly and its existence questioned, four decades later scientists discovered how to engineer negative Poisson's ratio into structures from molecular to macro scale. This has given rise to a new class of material termed 'auxetic'.

Auxetic materials are hierarchical cellular assemblies that demonstrate a negative Poisson's ratio thanks to the geometrical design of their cell units. When pulled, an auxetic structure becomes thicker in one or more perpendicular directions: in other words it becomes fatter when stretched rather than thinner as conventional materials do. There are numerous examples of auxetic biological materials, such as cow's udder, embryonic skins, artery tissue and even some bone structures.

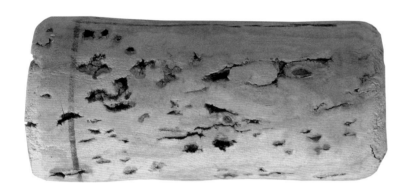

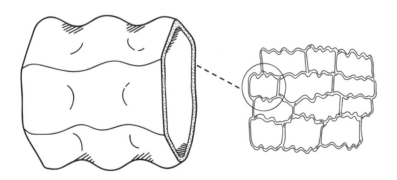

TOP A commercial cork stopper used to seal wine bottles.

ABOVE Illustration of cork cell structure from the side, showing the corrugated wall design responsible for cork's zero Poisson's ratio.

A regular hexagon-shaped cellular structure exposed to a force that causes bending – it curves in one direction.

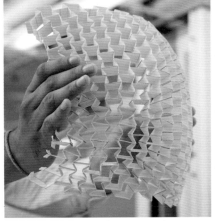

An auxetic cellular structure demonstrating synclastic curvature when exposed to a force – it becomes dome-shaped.

An auxetic cellular structure at rest.

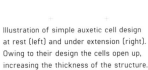

Illustration of simple auxetic cell design at rest (left) and under extension (right). Owing to their design the cells open up, increasing the thickness of the structure.

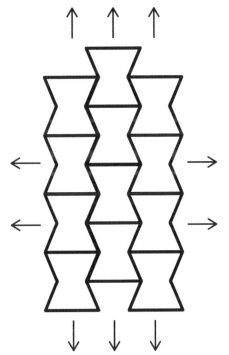

MAN-MADE AUXETIC STRUCTURES

In 1987, Roderick Lakes was the first to develop a method for retro-engineering auxetic structures into conventional foams by heating the material and allowing it to cool under pressure. Today, Professor Andrew Alderson from the UK's Sheffield Hallam University is a world-leading expert in the development of man-made auxetic structures. Alderson's group and its collaborators conduct extensive studies of auxetic behaviour in biological materials and have applied the resulting design principles to the creation of foams, textiles and composites from materials such as ceramics, metals, paper and plastics.

These structures have numerous industrial applications because they are tough, tear-resistant and highly compressible yet difficult to shear (break using sideways force) even when made from weaker materials such as paper. Furthermore, Alderson's team discovered that auxetic structures demonstrate a unique synclastic (dome-shape) curvature during bending, a characteristic that lends itself to the creation of simple shelters and tent-type structures.

Three examples of cellular auxetic structures.

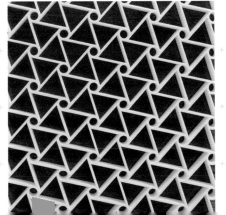

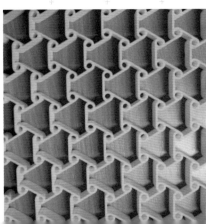

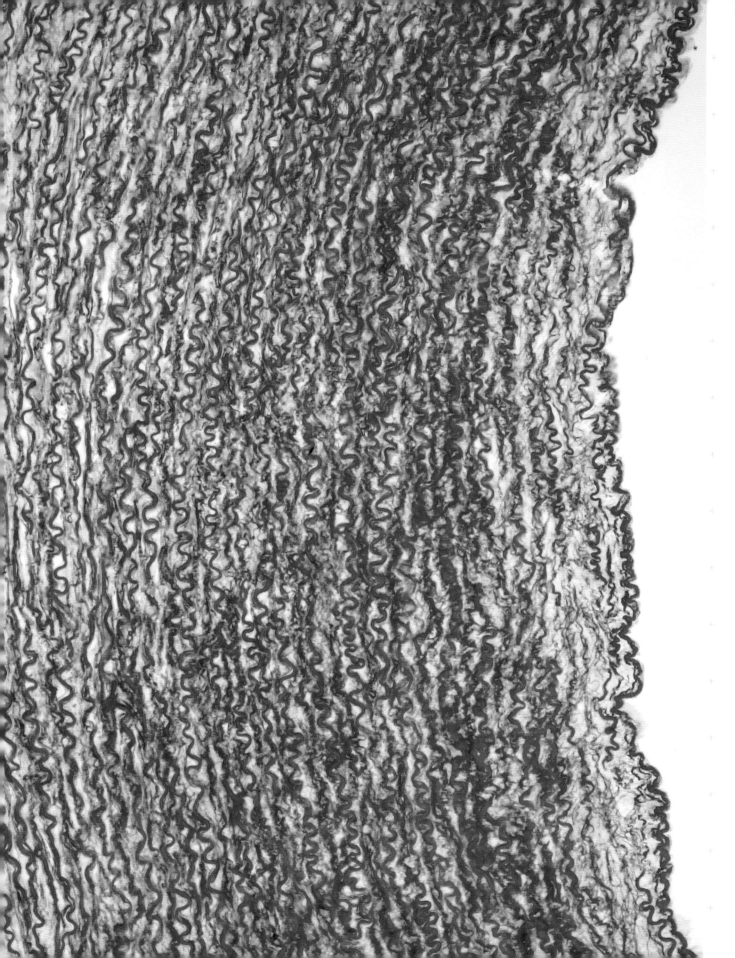

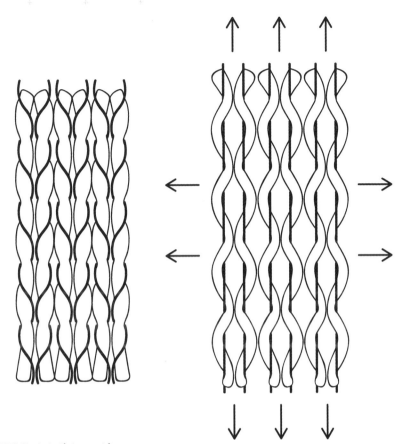

AUXETIC YARN

Auxetix Limited is an award-winning UK company that developed an auxetic yarn branded Zetix. The design, developed by Patrick Hook as part of his PhD studies at Exeter University in the UK, consists of a composite yarn made from two finer yarns, one elastic and one stiff, twisted into a helical formation. Normally an elastic yarn would become thinner as it was stretched; however, the Zetix configuration creates the opposite effect. The stiffer thread restricts and manages the stretch of the elastic component; under stress the elastic yarn becomes longer, but this shape change is limited locally to the area between two twists, causing a protrusion or a bow. The overall effect of this is a temporary thickening of the yarn and a negative Poisson's ratio.

The yarn has been incorporated into a woven textile proven to provide highly efficient protection from blast particles. During ballistic impact the structure is able to deform without breaking and dissipate energy over a large area involving many fibres, which allows the capture of shrapnel. Thousands of pores open up over the surface during impact to 'vent' blast waves, while the elastic core of the yarns does not fracture like conventional ballistic-resistant textiles. This technology has been applied to the design of a blast-resistant curtain that can capture debris such as glass, protecting individuals working or living in buildings within conflict areas. Other applications range from aerospace to smart textile sensors for architecture and interiors.

OPPOSITE Histological (microscopic) section of an elastic artery in the human aorta. Some artery cells have auxetic structures.

ABOVE Illustration of auxetic yarn functionality: in relaxed state (left), and exposed to extension forces similar to those from blast waves (right). Thanks to the design of the yarn composite, the structure 'opens up' and becomes wider.

BELOW Auxetic foam at rest (left) and exposed to extension forces (right). The structure increases in width significantly when stretched.

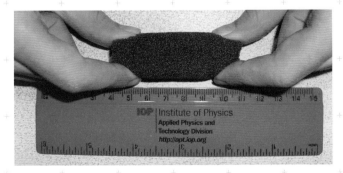

ABOVE The stump of a freshly cut tree; a chainsaw creates a partial cut and the tree is left to collapse – as it does so the wood fibres are torn individually.

FAR LEFT Close-up of a tree stump, with marks from the chainsaw and from where the tree tore when it fell.

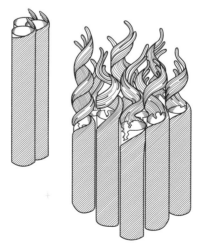

ABOVE Illustration of torn wood fibres showing the orientation of cellulose microfibrils.

Professor George Jeronimidis, an engineer and one of the founders of biomimetics in the UK (see p.11), was fascinated by the properties of wood. During his early career in the late 1970s Jeronimidis collaborated with the inspirational Jim Gordon (author of *The New Science of Strong Materials*) to understand why wood was tougher (resisting cracking) than it should be based on the knowledge and understanding at the time. Wood is a fibrous material made from tiny strawlike tubes (wood fibres) that run in parallel to the length of the tree and are tightly packed together. The cell walls are made of cellulose nanofibres arranged at a 15-degree angle to the axis of the cell.

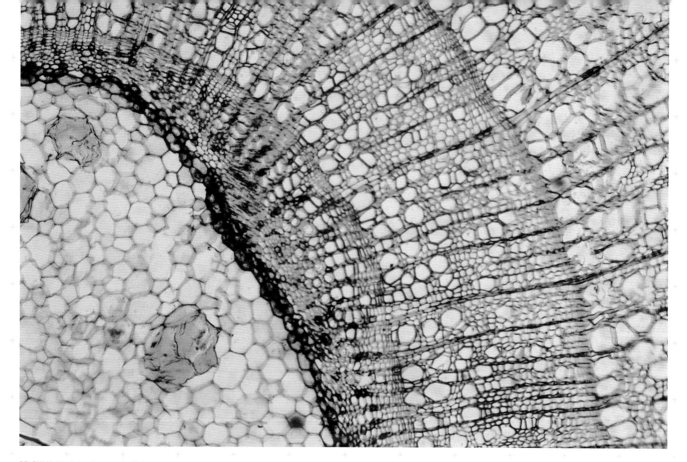

BELOW Light photomicrograph of pine wood cross-section seen through a microscope, with close-up (above).

BIOMIMETIC WOOD

Following a series of observations and analysis, Jeronimidis created a model of wood by making a series of tubes using glass fibres wound round a nylon core at 15 degrees and set in resin. Once the resin had hardened the core was removed and the tubes glued together. Experiments on this model revealed that when the tubes were bent to breaking point, first individual tube walls buckled inward, then the resin holding the fibres together cracked, but the glass fibre was left intact. Furthermore, as the glass fibres were still intact, the structure was able to stretch a bit more, thus demonstrating remarkable ductile (pliable) behaviour although being made exclusively of brittle materials. Jeronimidis designed several versions of composite structures using this design principle and produced materials that were cheaper yet five times tougher, weight for weight, than steel.

These prototypes were developed in the 1980s, and at that time the routes to commercial production were not obvious. Today, with advances in digital manufacturing methods, there are numerous ways in which this material could be developed into a commercial-scale product. Textile technology is one possibility.

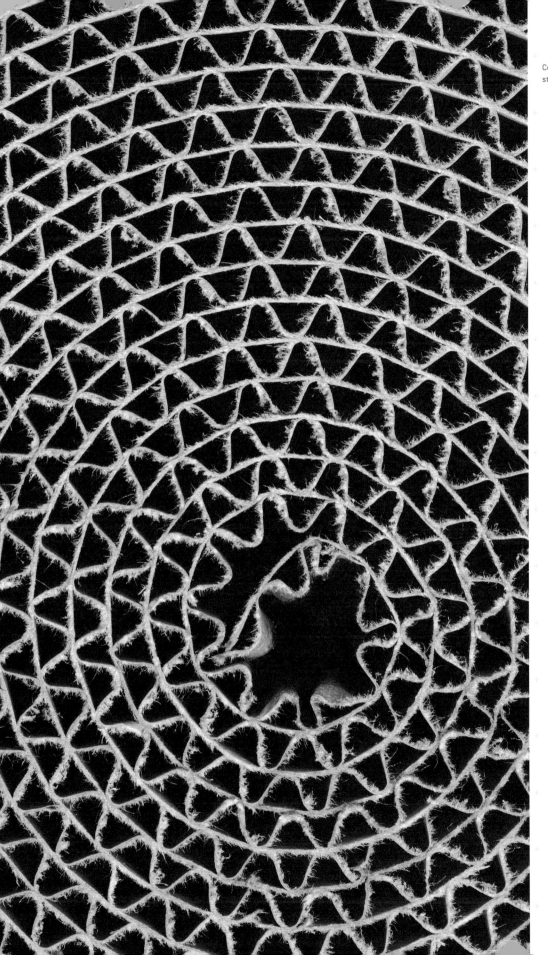

Corrugated cardboard, which has a similar structure to that of biomimetic wood.

RIGHT AND BELOW Close-up of bullet impact point in biomimetic wood sample. Damage from impact is nominal, with no cracks forming and the structure remaining functional.

BOTTOM Section view of wood cells under microscope.

NACRE

Tough by design

SYNTHETIC NACRE

Superfine yet tough shells

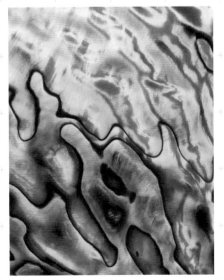

The remarkably strong shell of the abalone
(above) has a dull, ridged exterior, while
the interior is lined with an iridescent
layer (detail, left).

Molluscs have shells whose primary function is to protect the fragile body of the animal within from foreign objects and predators. The inner shell layer of some molluscs, such as the abalone and the pearl oyster, is lined with an iridescent material known as mother-of-pearl, or nacre. Nacre is composed of 98 per cent calcium carbonate mineral, which makes it stiff and hard, and 2 per cent protein, yet it demonstrates a level of toughness (resistance to cracking) 3,000 times greater than the mineral it is made from.

This is due to the way the material is organized at nano scale. Nacre is a hierarchical structure; the calcium carbonate forms individual microscopic polygonal plates (5–15 microns wide, 1–5 microns thick) stacked like bricks, sometimes in columns like walls and sometimes like random tiles. The calcium carbonate plates have the ability to slide along one another under tension. Just like wood (see p.104), this system has a ductile property that is responsible for the highly amplified toughness and tolerance to damage.

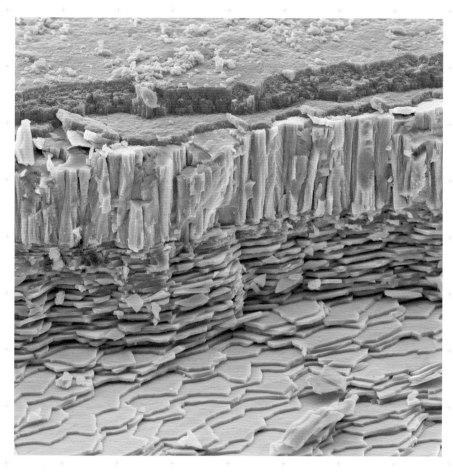

LEFT Coloured scanning electron micrograph (SEM) of a section through an abalone shell. The majority of the shell is composed of layers of overlapping platelets of calcium carbonate crystals, or aragonite (grey). Between the layers are thin sheets of protein (not seen). This structure makes the shell much stronger than the materials would be in any other arrangement.

BELOW Illustration of the mechanism responsible for the shell's advanced properties. Overlapping platelets of calcium carbonate crystals slide over each other under pressure, dissipating the force of impact.

SYNTHETIC NACRE

Although still experimental, synthetic nacre promises to be an important material in the future, with applications spanning from medical to jewelry, and possibilities in introducing this mechanism at large scales for applications in architecture, interiors and consumer products.

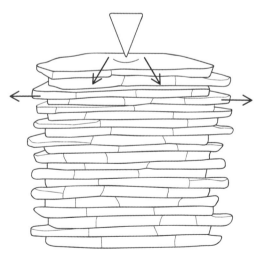

DINOSAUR EEL

Bite-resistant scales

METAMESH

New-generation mail armour

The skin of the Senegal bichir, or 'dinosaur eel', serves as extremely effective armour.

Ninety-six million years ago, most fish would have been covered in a tough, penetration-resistant dermal armour as protection against the number of large invertebrate predators with razor-sharp teeth that populated the lakes and oceans. Today, with significantly fewer such predators, this prehistoric defence mechanism has been largely phased out. Unlike its aquatic contemporaries, the Senegal bichir (*Polypterus senegalus*), a fish that inhabits muddy freshwater pools in Africa, retains its ancient dermal armour, hence its popular name of 'dinosaur

eel'. In fact, *P. senegalus* has undergone very few structural or behavioural changes over the last ninety million years and retains close links to its ancestors. Unlike other fish species that lost their protective skins as their predators disappeared, the cannibalistic nature of the dinosaur eel means that its main predator remains at large.

In 2008, the US Department of Defense funded an expert team led by Christine Ortiz at Massachusetts Institute of Technology (MIT) to conduct a nano-scale analysis of the animal's dermal armour system. The team found a

hierarchical structure consisting of scales 500 microns thick and a highly specialized scale geometry that varies along the length of the animal's body. The outer surface of the scale is approximately 10 microns thick and composed of guanine, a very hard, enamel-like material, followed by 50 microns of dentine, 40 microns of a bonelike substance called isopedine and 300 microns of a bone basal plate. When the fish is attacked, the top, stiff guanine layer transfers load to the softer dentine layer, which dissipates energy; during high-energy attacks resulting in

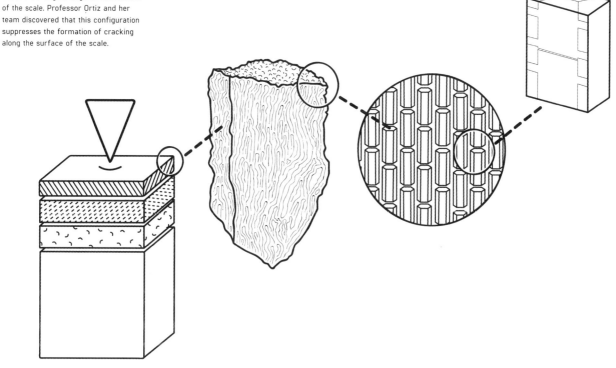

BELOW Illustration showing the four-layer structure of the dinosaur eel scale. The top, external layer of guanine is composed of tiny rodlike nanocrystals aligned at about a 90-degree angle to the surface of the scale. Professor Ortiz and her team discovered that this configuration suppresses the formation of cracking along the surface of the scale.

deep penetrations, the isopedine layer forms microscopic cracks that minimize impact across the overall structure.

Analysis of the scale geometry revealed that each scale consists of two regions – a flap-type area that forms overlapping joints to cover skin and allow bending and sliding to accommodate body movement, and a unique peg-and-joint system that interlocks the scales into a structure and connects them to the skin.

METAMESH

The team is currently working on transferring these findings to the design of advanced lightweight modular armour surfaces for soldiers as an alternative to the larger protective plates used currently, which impede movement. The project, titled MetaMesh, explores how to design scaled armour systems that work with the contours of a human body without obstructing motion. In addition to defence applications, this type of textile structure would be hugely beneficial to specialist garments for activities involving deliberate or accidental impact.

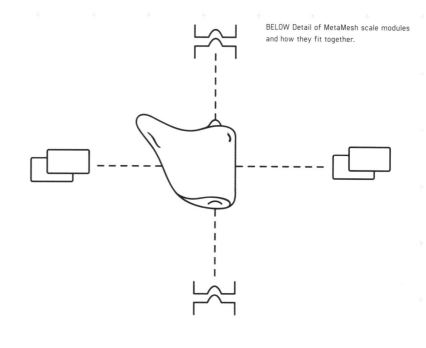

BELOW Detail of MetaMesh scale modules and how they fit together.

BIOMIMETIC APPLICATION

ADVANCED PROTECTIVE EQUIPMENT

Lightweight impact-resistant systems

The scaly-foot snail (*Crysomallon squamiferum*) was recently discovered in the deep-sea volcanic vents of the Central Indian Ridge, one of the most hostile environments on Earth. The snail has evolved a remarkable exoskeletal structure that enables survival in such extreme conditions as well as resistance to attack from its main

predator, the crab. Once a crab catches a snail in its claw, it can squeeze it for days if necessary. However, thanks to the unique structure of the snail shell, the animal is able to withstand prolonged compression.

The scaly-foot snail has been found at depths of 2,400 metres (7,870 feet).

Commercial bicycle helmets are currently made from a foam with an external coating of stiff polymer and an internal lining of polyester-type fabric. This type of protective product would significantly benefit from the development of an advanced protective system inspired by the scaly-foot snail.

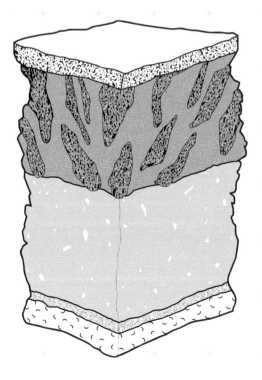

PROTECTIVE EQUIPMENT

Christine Ortiz at the Massachusetts Institute of Technology (MIT) leads the team working on understanding how the snail shell works. The team applied techniques that simulated the squeezing motion of the crab and discovered a structure consisting of three layers: two stiff mineralized layers with a thick organic layer sandwiched between them. The team is working on transferring this knowledge and understanding to the design of composite materials with a range of applications from body armour to vehicle exteriors. Other applications are as components in civilian protective equipment such as bicycle and motorcycle helmets, pads and so on.

The shell's outer layer consists of iron sulphides, the middle layer is equivalent to the organic periostracum (horny covering) found in other gastropods, and the innermost layer is made of aragonite (calcium carbonate).

SEAHORSE SKELETON

Resilient by design

RESILIENT STRUCTURES

Advanced impact protection

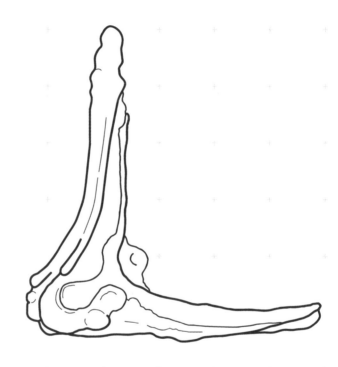

The seahorse (*Hippocampus*) has many predators, including sea turtles, crabs and birds, which capture the animals and crush them. Their only line of defence is their tail, which is used to hook on to corals or seaweed to hide from predators.

A research group led by Joanna McKittrick and Marc Meyers from the Jacobs School of Engineering at the University of California, San Diego, found that the seahorse tail functions as a remarkable armour that protects the animal's spinal cord from compression during attack. The team calculated that the structure could be compressed from various angles up to 50 per cent of its original width without causing any damage to the seahorse's spinal column; even 60 per cent compression left no permanent damage.

Study of the tail-bone composition revealed 27 per cent organic compounds (mostly proteins) and 33 per cent water, and a surprisingly low volume of minerals, responsible for stiffness – about 40 per cent, as compared to 65 per cent in cow bone. This means that the material alone is not sufficient to withstand significant compressive forces. Analysis of the tail's skeletal structure revealed a system of thirty-six square-like segments, each composed of four L-shaped corner plates that gradually decrease in size along the length of the tail. The team concluded that the remarkable compressive properties of the seahorse tail were due to the design of the skeletal system, with each corner plate designed to slide past adjacent plates under compression rather than break or snap.

ABOVE Illustration of one of the four L-shaped corner plates that form a segment of the seahorse tail skeleton.

LEFT A seahorse with its curled prehensile tail.

ABOVE American football shoulder padding is a type of protective garment that could benefit from the biomimetic seahorse structure.

RIGHT Illustration of the thirty-six connected square segments that form the seahorse tail skeleton.

RESILIENT STRUCTURES

The team plans to use 3D printing to create an artificial bony plate system to make flexible yet robust robotic arms or grippers for medical devices, underwater exploration and unmanned bomb detection and detonation. This type of resilient modular structure has numerous applications in consumer products, from advanced packaging and mobile device casings to protective gear for extreme sports.

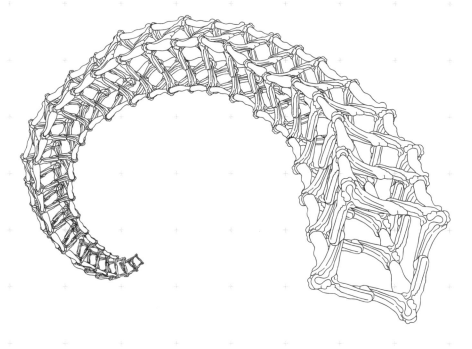

GLASS SPONGE

Nature's skyscrapers

BIOGLASS-INSPIRED STRUCTURES

Hierarchical lightweight functional systems

ABOVE Detail of the top of the sponge.

LEFT A deep-sea glass sponge anchored to the ocean floor.

Sponges are skeletal structures made from microscopic fibres, or spicules, composed of proteins (stretchy) and minerals (brittle). The deep-sea sponge *Euplectella aspergillum* dwells in the western Pacific Ocean, loosely anchored to the soft sediment of the ocean floor; it is known as 'Venus's flower basket' because it is often occupied by a pair of mated shrimp. The sponge, 20–25 centimetres (7.8–9.8 inches) long and 2–4 centimetres (0.8–1.6 inches) in diameter, filters minute particles of food from the water that passes through its cylindrical cagelike structure. *E. aspergillum* is what is known as a glass sponge, and its structure consists of a rigid, complex latticework of spicules composed mainly of glass (silica), yet demonstrating an exceptional toughness that enables the organism to withstand external forces such as the ocean current and impact from foreign objects or marine animals.

Glass is notoriously fragile, yet is used widely as a building material: this paradox between system function and material properties is compensated for by design. A team of researchers led by Dr Joanna Aizenberg of Harvard University's Wyss

Institute for Biologically Inspired Engineering compared the flexibility and toughness of the glass sponge spicules with synthetic glass rods of similar length and found that the biological material demonstrated remarkable resilience when compared to its brittle man-made analogue. The team conducted an in-depth analysis of the sponge from the nano to the macro scale and discovered a complex structure revealing several levels of hierarchy.

During the early stages of formation, the spicules are composed of a protein filament core coated in layers of silica nanospheres (forming a bioglass layer – brittle) and organic material (protein – elastic). The intermittent layers of brittle and elastic material deliver a system that can prevent it from cracking when bent. The spicules are fused into parallel bundles and arranged in a square-grid cylinder reinforced by diagonal fibres running in both directions. The compound effect of fibre bundles greatly increases the resilience of the system when compared to individual fibres. As the sponge structure matures, the flexible spicules of skeletal lattice are coated in silica cement that transforms into a stiff sponge. The elongated cylindrical basket shape also offers enhanced stability.

RIGHT Glass sponge.

BELOW Illustration of the hierarchical
structure of the glass sponge: parallel
bundles of spicules of protein filament
core coated in silica nanospheres are
arranged in a square-grid cylinder
reinforced by diagonal fibres.

BOTTOM Illustration of the type of
structures that could be made from
a bioglass-type system.

ADVANCED STRUCTURES

Aizenberg's team concluded that the exceptional
properties of the skeleton are due to the design
and assembly of the glass from the nano to the
macro scale. This discovery can inform the design
of advanced structures demonstrating properties
that are counterintuitive for glass, such as ductility
(enabling it to withstand cracks), resulting in
applications not currently associated with glass
in a variety of industries including architecture,
interiors, vehicles and the medical sector.

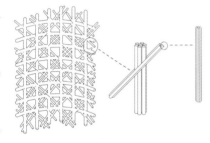

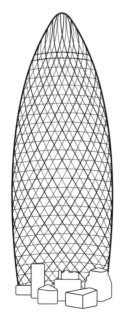

POLAR BEAR FUR | SOLAR TEXTILES

Functional fur design | Advanced thermal textiles

Polar bears are among the largest predators on the planet, yet they inhabit a harsh and isolated Arctic environment, surviving in temperatures as low as -50°C (-58°F). Their characteristic white coats offer camouflage – but also constitute the primary mechanism that enables survival in such harsh conditions.

The primary mechanism that enables the bears to survive in extreme conditions consists of a dense layer of fat lining the animal's skin – up to 10 centimetres (4 inches) thick – combined with specialized hairs. The longer hairs are translucent and demonstrate a unique design, resembling a hollow fibre, but instead of a void, the core houses a type of cellular structure. Polar bear skin is black, which fuelled a controversial myth suggesting that the hairs of the polar bear fur functioned like a type of fibre-optic tubing capable of drawing sunlight to the skin, which, thanks to its colour, absorbed the light. Physicist Daniel W. Koon and his graduate assistant Reid Hutchins refuted this theory in 1988.

Twenty years later a team of biomimetic scientists, led by Thomas Stegmaier from Germany's Institute of Textile Technology and Process Engineering (ITV), Denkendorf, conducted a study of polar bear fur. The team discovered that polar bears are nearly invisible when observed with an infrared camera, which makes heat radiation visible to the human eye. Stegmaier and his team concluded that radiation from the sun travels through the fur towards the skin but is not lost by convection, and thus the fur functions like a type of solar trap.

RIGHT A textile developed by
SolarEnergie Stefanakis.

BELOW An example of a solar thermal
collector for which SolarEnergie covers
could be beneficial, helping to retain
the heat.

SOLAR TEXTILES

Stegmaier joined forces with industrial partner
SolarEnergie Stefanakis to develop a system
capable of mimicking these properties. Initially
the group attempted to create a synthetic
fur; however, this format was not suitable for
industrial energy-harvesting applications, so
the team reviewed the design and applied the
principles to the development of a composite
cellular textile system. This biomimetic textile
is currently applied as soft, flexible covers for
SolarEnergie Stefanakis water desalination and
energy-harvesting products that offer thermal
insulation with additional heat generation,
evaporation and air-cooling properties.

PLANT ROOTS

Large-scale moisture management

TRANSPIRATIONAL TEXTILES

Engineered structural wicking

Part-exposed tree-root system.

Plants have evolved gravity-defying strategies for drawing water and nutrients from the soil up into the stem, branches and leaves without the aid of a mechanical pumping system. Liquid water from the ground is absorbed by a plant's roots and distributed up the stem to the branches and leaves through microscopic tubes known as xylem. When water reaches the leaf, it is held on the surface of specialized spongy cells inside the leaf and diffuses out into the environment via the leaf's stomata (pores) in a process known as transpiration. The loss of moisture through transpiration creates internal negative pressure within the xylem tubes, like a drinking straw, allowing water to be sucked up through the roots to the leaves. The branching structure of plant root networks plays a significant role in optimizing transpiration, since the large surface areas of roots allow nutrient-containing fluid to flow with minimum resistance.

Onion plant with an extensive system of underground roots.

TRANSPIRATIONAL TEXTILES

This design principle inspired Qing Chen, a doctoral student from Hong Kong's Institute of Textiles and Clothing, to design and develop a transpirational textile system drawing on the morphology of plant root systems. Chen's concept uses the capillary action of wicking fibres to simulate the negative pressure strategy used by plants, and focuses on the morphology of branching root systems. Wicking fibres have a characteristic cross-section: instead of being round they feature lobar designs, often described as Mickey Mouse ears. Moisture is trapped in the lobe crevasses and capillary action draws the moisture upwards along the length of the fibre. These fibres are usually oriented in parallel to the fabric face; however, using cotton yarns in the warp and wicking polyester yarns such as Coolmax in the weft, Chen used advanced weaving technology to engineer multilayered textiles that allowed the weft yarns to travel through the layers of the textile from the inner to the outer layer to resemble root branching networks. This enabled the wicking fibres to be directed at right angles to the fabric face and travel through the various layers.

Experimental study of the properties demonstrated by these novel textiles showed quicker water transport and moisture management when compared to similar layered textiles without the novel structure. Applications for this type of textile vary from comfort and performance apparel to architecture and interior design.

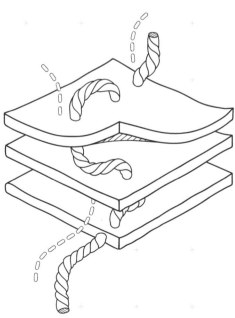

Illustration of transpirational textile concept: wicking yarns are applied in a three-dimensional system by travelling through multiple layers of cloth.

04

BIOLOGY

MAKING

The modern built environment is composed of a plethora of 'stuff' – articles and objects made for a variety of purposes, be it decoration, protection, shelter or tools. Stuff is *made*, usually through complex industrial processes that involve manipulating, combining and shaping materials. Many of our products, for example, are made from polymers – long strings of molecules made from smaller components called monomers. Conversely, stuff in nature is *grown*: organisms create their own materials and structures, also from lengthy polymer chains. These stringy molecules are incredibly important to both technology and biology because the way these chains interact, tangle or form knots determines the properties of the material such as strength, toughness and elasticity.

In order to create polymers it is necessary to encourage monomers to form links; the way humans do this is very different from biology's approach. Technology uses brute force to forge links between monomers by exposing them to high temperatures and pressures, a method born during the Industrial Revolution. The materials emerging from this transformation of non-renewable sources using toxic, energy-rich methods require similar conditions to decompose, which contributes greatly to our ever-increasing production of waste. Polymers in nature are formed in ambient conditions using minimum amounts of energy from abundant raw materials; equally, these materials decompose relatively easily and are redistributed into the system for reuse.

The key difference between natural and man-made polymers is information. Chapter 3 explored the impact of hierarchical design in biological systems; information in nature is expressed through form and structure from nano to macro scale. DNA is an iconic example of information-rich polymers: slight differences in connections between the molecule's double helix are what makes us physically different from each other. The structure of man-made polymers is much simpler; they are often made from the same repeating monomer. Slight changes to the order of building blocks within in a particular sequence will not result in any significant change to the material properties.

A return to pre-industrial practice is not the answer: a new paradigm for manufacture is essential and it involves *rethinking the way we make things*. In 2002, Michael Braungart and William McDonough published *Cradle to Cradle: Remaking the Way We Make Things*, a key text in sustainable design and manufacture that describes alternative ways of making things and includes ideas such as respecting diversity and regarding waste as food. Biomimetics can support the path towards what is known as a cradle-to-cradle approach by offering both conceptual and practical strategies, including ways of creating information-rich materials that transcend the current digital/physical boundaries and advanced sustainable technologies for manufacture.

OPPOSITE Industrial-scale processing of steel involves melting of metals to liquid state; cast iron melts at 1375°C (2507°F).

RIGHT A seedling newly sprouted from a seed; environmental conditions that enable germination are water, oxygen and an ambient temperature ranging from 16 to 32°C (60 to 90°F) depending on species.

PAPER WASP

Structures from macerated wood fibres

PAPER INDUSTRY

Products from wood pulp

In the early seventeenth century, French naturalist and entomologist René-Antoine Réaumur conducted the first ever study on wasps. During observations of the North American genus *Polistes*, Réaumur noticed the fine paper-like quality of the material the wasps produced to construct hives. Papermaking technology dates back to *c.* 4000 BCE in ancient Egypt, where sheets of papyrus were made by weaving and drying the inner pith of the papyrus plant. The first method for making paper from cellulose pulp extracted from mulberry leaves and cotton linter was developed in China during the Han Dynasty (206 BCE – 220 CE). In Réaumur's time, the quality of paper was thick and coarse compared to paper today, because cotton and linen rag formed the raw material for paper manufacture. Paper in the seventeenth century was also greatly expensive owing to the competition for raw materials from the textile industry.

TOP Paper wasps gather fibres from dead wood and plant stems, which they mix with saliva and use to construct water-resistant nests made of papery material.

ABOVE An egg carton of recycled paper pulp, a common packaging material made into products using a mechanized papier mâché ('chewed paper') process.

ABOVE A Freedom of Creation 3D-printed wood structure made from sawdust and adhesive.

RIGHT Freedom of Creation 3D-printed wood products.

PAPER FROM WOOD

In 1719, Réaumur noted in his article *Histoire des Guêpes* (History of Wasps) that the wasp was able to make paper from wood by macerating it and gluing it into fine sheets without the use of rags and linens. He recognized the opportunity presented by the wasp's mechanism as a great technological challenge that could revolutionize the papermaking industry. Over the following century, Réaumur's observations sparked a series of innovations that led to the transition of raw material from rag to wood pulp, which enabled the cheap, mass production of paper products, including the fine sheets of paper we use today.

3D-PRINTED WOOD

Wood is one of the more sustainable and renewable sources of material; wood pulp can be used to create a range of disposable, biodegradable products for packaging; however, wood pulp as a material for creating 3D objects has limited aesthetic and mechanical properties.

ABOVE Fine continuous sheets of paper during processing in a modern pulp mill.

BELOW A hornet sitting on its vespiary, or nest.

In 1719, the idea of additive manufacturing had not yet been conceived; had Réaumur been able to look into a crystal ball he would have drawn further parallels between the paper wasp and freeform additive manufacturing (3D-printing) systems. Essentially, the insect creates its own material by combining a type of mucus with ground wood tissue, and deposits it bit by bit to form a 3D shelter.

In 2009, Dutch 3D-printing pioneers Freedom of Creation set out to develop ways to introduce wood into additive manufacture. The team began to experiment with sawdust and binder as part of a project titled 'tree-d printing'. By 2011 they were able to create objects from sawdust, a byproduct of the wood industry. Although there is more work to be done to optimize the processing and the nature of the binder, which is currently a type of plastic, advances in additive manufacturing enable the creation of 3D structures by regenerating waste material, in this case sawdust.

RIGHT Close-up of a wasp on its fine papery nest.

BELOW Freedom of Creation post-production hand-processing of 3D-printed wood object.

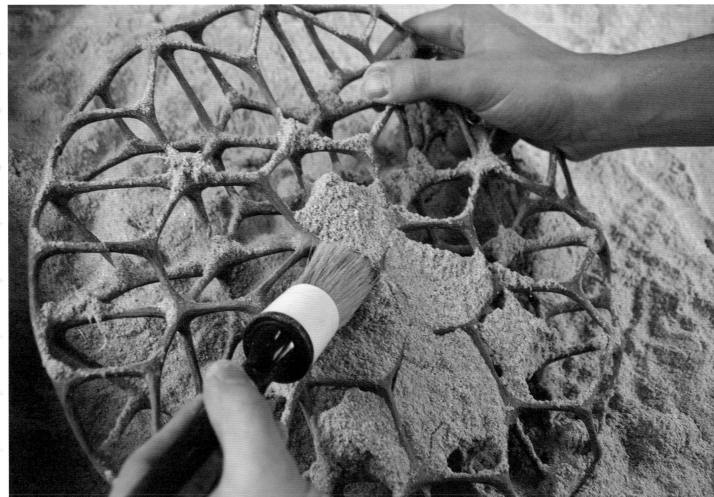

COCOON SILK

Insect fibre-extrusion mechanisms

MAN-MADE FIBRE
INDUSTRY

Regenerated and synthetic fibres

An adult silkworm moth. It takes more
than 5,000 silkworms to make 1 kg
(2.2 lb) of raw silk.

Silk is a natural fibre created by a number of insects such as spiders, moths and bees. Solutions of amino acids are produced inside the insect's body and extruded through microscopic holes, where the material solidifies on contact with air. This unique process enables the creation of long, fine fibres of continuous, uninterrupted filaments. The domesticated silk moth, *Bombyx mori*, is the most common insect employed in silk production, or sericulture. Centuries or even millennia of selective breeding have resulted in the generation of a moth that

has lost its ability to see and fly and is capable only of mating and egg production for sericulture.

The true origins of silk production remain unknown; it is believed that the technology for production and processing of silk evolved around 3000 BCE in China, although archaeological findings along the Yangtze River have revealed tools and other artefacts relevant to sericulture dating to before 7000 BCE.

Silk production was highly valued by the Chinese and remained a carefully guarded secret for thousands of years. Attempts to leak

information out of the country were considered treason and punished by death. The unique properties of the fibres – lustrous and fine yet very robust – made silk a precious commodity. A few fibres could be spun together to form a thin yarn strong enough to be processed into a fine, semitransparent cloth impossible to recreate using any other natural fibre.

ABOVE A silkworm moth emerging from its cocoon. As this breaks the long single filament, in commercial production the cocoons are boiled to kill the pupae before the moth can emerge.

RIGHT Before the era of man-made fibres: women working at textile machines in Boston, Massachusetts, c.1910.

MAN-MADE SILK

Attempts by the Chinese to create a synthetic version of the fibre are believed to date as far back as 3000 BCE. However, it took thousands of years to develop the technology able to deliver fine filament fibres on a commercial scale, an event that marked the birth of the man-made fibre industry. Rayon (or viscose) was the first man-made fibre, commercially produced by the British silk firm Courtauld's in 1905; it echoed the lustre of silk but lacked its strength. This property was achieved with the invention and consequent mass production from 1939 of nylon, a polyamide, by DuPont, which was used during the war and famously went on to revolutionize fashion in the 1950s. Cheap super-lightweight nylon stockings rapidly superseded their exclusive silk counterparts and were accessible to a wider demographic. In 1969, as Neil Armstrong took 'one small step for [a] man, one giant leap for mankind', he planted a nylon flag on the surface of the moon in a suit made from thirty layers of nylon and aramid fibres.

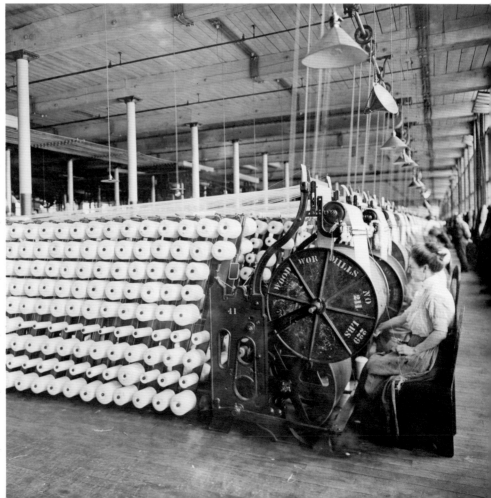

RIGHT Yarn spools on a spinning machine in a textile factory.

BELOW Baskets of silkworm cocoons at a silk factory. Each cocoon consists of up to about 900 m (3,000 ft) of continuous silk filament.

Today the man-made fibre industry is growing; global turnover had risen to 1.65 billion US dollars in 2013. Although fibres such as nylon and Kevlar are comparable in terms of strength to cocoon silk and have valuable properties, they require a huge amount of energy (heat and pressure), toxic chemicals and resources (fossil fuels) to produce, and are difficult to recycle. *Bombyx mori* and other silk-producing insects create biodegradable fibres in ambient conditions by drawing on the resources available to them in their environment, be it leaves or other insects. The importance of the man-made fibre industry is without question; however, are there other ways of creating fibres that are more energy-efficient and sustainable?

Rayon belongs to a class of fibre made from regenerated polymers (fibres made from naturally occurring polymers such as cellulose), which preceded their synthetic counterparts (made from polymers that do not exist in nature). Although wood pulp, the raw material used in rayon production, is considered a sustainable source, processing it into fibres requires toxic chemicals. Austrian company Lenzing, which produces 25 per cent of the world's rayon fibres, has invested in cleaning up production by developing closed-loop industrial processes to enable the retention and reuse of chemicals.

More recently, bamboo – one of the world's fastest-growing plants, which can reach growth rates of more than 10 centimetres (4 inches) per hour – has been developed as an alternative source. Regenerated cellulose fibres are hygroscopic (absorb moisture), a property that makes the fibres attractive for next-to-skin garments and hygiene products; however, there are many applications where hydrophobic (no interaction with water) properties are necessary, a common characteristic of synthetics.

Biopolymers such as polylactic acid (PLA), a material derived from the fermentation of corn and sugar beet, can demonstrate similar strength to synthetic plastics and presents a promising alternative. PLA has a lower melting point than polyamide and polyester and can thus be processed at lower temperatures using conventional industrial equipment. Although there are questions about biodegradability, PLA is currently used in packaging, non-disposable products and textiles.

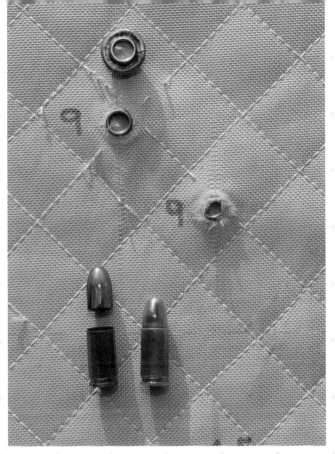

ABOVE A Kevlar bulletproof vest shot with 9 mm bullets. Silk is of comparable strength to Kevlar but requires far fewer resources to produce.

ABOVE RIGHT Cocoons range in colour from white to golden yellow.

RIGHT An industrial knitting machine.

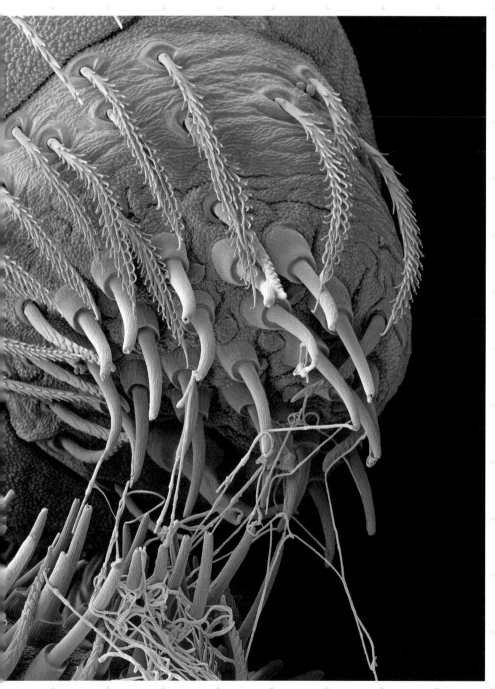

BIOLOGY

SPIDER SILK

Multifunctional fibres in ambient conditions

BIOMIMETIC APPLICATION

SYNTHETIC
SPIDER SILK

Man-made protein fibres with tailorable properties

The extraordinary properties of spider silk have benefited humankind for centuries. The ancient Greeks are known to have applied sheets of spider web to open wounds, where the antiseptic properties would prevent infection and encourage healing; furthermore, the silk was absorbed by the body and functioned as a type of graft. Spider silk was also used for the crosshairs of early optical instruments such as microscopes and telescopes.

It is possible to harvest silk fibres directly from the spider using a method known as milking. However, farming spiders is a near-impossible task; spiders are notoriously territorial animals prone to killing each other in confined spaces. Professor Fritz Vollrath, a world-leading expert in spider silk, has successfully managed to create a spider farm on the top of the zoology building at Oxford University in the UK and sometimes uses the livestock for milking. Vollrath estimates the value of harvested spider silk at $150,000 per kilo, compared to approximately $10 per kilo for cocoon silk.

In 2004, textile designer Simon Peers and entrepreneur Nicholas Godley embarked on an unusual quest to farm spiders and harvest their silk for the production of textiles. The idea for this project was triggered by the discovery of a reproduction antique spider-milking machine in Peers's office in Madagascar. Further research revealed that French missionaries attempted to harvest spider silk in the late nineteenth century, but owing to the complex nature of the processes involved they were able to produce enough fibre for only a few pieces. Peers and Godley remained undeterred and set out to explore this process themselves. After eight years and milking more than a million golden orb spiders the pair produced a cape made from 100 per cent golden orb spider silk. The extraordinary saffron colour is due to the nature of the fibres. The total cost of this endeavour was in the region of £300,000 and demonstrated that farming spiders for silk is not a commercially viable process.

LEFT Coloured scanning electron micrograph (SEM) of the end of a spider's abdomen showing silk threads being produced by a spinneret. Spider silk is very elastic and can be stretched 30–40 per cent of its length before it breaks.

LEFT An orb spider spinning a web.

CENTRE An orb spider creating a decorative pattern on its web; the function of this behaviour is not fully understood.

BELOW The spinnerets on a giant house spider.

SYNTHETIC SPIDER SILK

Arachnids have evolved a remarkable ability to produce different types of silk. The garden spider uses silk not only to form webs but to suspend itself, wrap prey and create protective enclosures. Golden orb spiders can produce seven types of silk with different properties including sticky, strong, stretchy and cement-like. Spider silk is made from a protein solution and consists of characteristically long molecules with repeating patterns of non-essential amino acids glycine and alanine (essential amino acids are classified as those that cannot be produced by the organism and are introduced through diet alone, non-essential amino acids are produced in the body). Golden orb spiders can engineer a range of properties in the fibres they extrude by managing the microstructure of the fibre polymer in ambient conditions during extrusion.

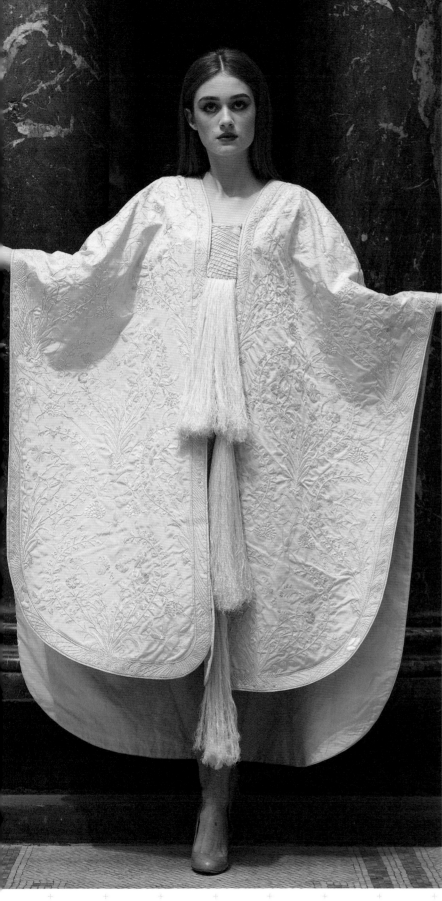

LEFT Bianca Gavrilas models a hand-
embroidered cape made by Nicholas
Godley and Simon Peers from the naturally
golden silk of the orb spider, at the
Victoria and Albert Museum, London, 2012.

During the 1990s Fritz Vollrath and his team
at Oxford University conducted basic research
into the spider's silk production mechanisms
and discovered that they were able to control the
folding and crystallization of the main protein
constituents by adding auxiliary compounds
to create a composite material of defined
hierarchical structure. The spinning dope
(the material from which silk is spun) is liquid
crystalline, and during extrusion spiders can
draw it into a hardened fibre using minimal force.
This involves a double drawing process: one
that occurs internally, followed by an external
drawdown after the dope has left the spinneret.
Vollrath applied this knowledge to form the basis
for the design of a biomimetic fibre spinning
machine in 2001 that imitates the spider's
internal processing and control over protein
folding combined with the knowledge of gene
sequencing of its spinning dopes.

The German company Spintec Engineering
GmbH has set up a commercial-scale version of
the biomimetic silk spinning facility, applying it
to the development and production of innovative
medical devices for wound therapy and dental
and surgical implants. This novel fibre-extruding
technology has the potential to introduce
information into fibre structure and enable the
engineering of finely tuned filaments for a range
of industries from automotive and apparel to
medical and space.

ABOVE A dental prosthetic
holding two false teeth. Currently
made from polymethylmethacrylate
acrylic (PMMA), in the future this could
be replaced by biomimetic silk.

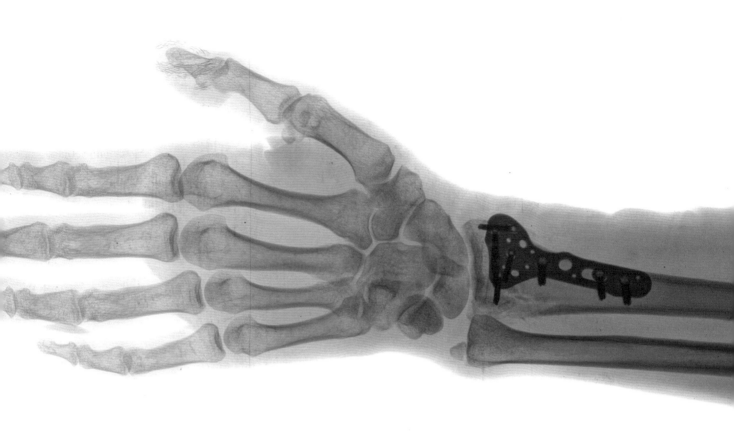

LEFT Spinneret of wolf spider.

BELOW Biomedical plates made from surgical-grade stainless steel used for implants, surgical equipment, body piercing jewelry and body modification implants; in the future biomimetic silk could replace metal alloys used in body applications, including the metallic implant seen in the x-ray image of the hand (above).

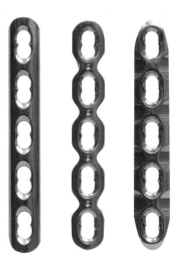

BIOLOGY

BACTERIAL SILK

Low-energy microbial factories

BIOMIMETIC APPLICATION

BOLT THREADS

Fermentation versus high-energy reactions

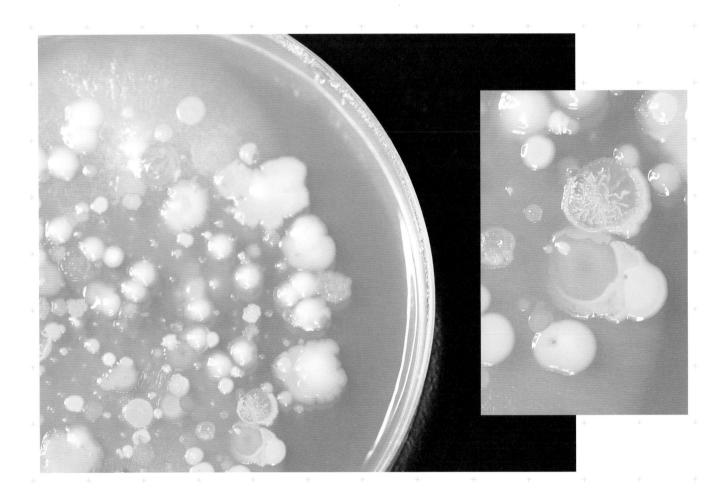

Bacterial colonies growing in a
petri dish on agar.

The early twentieth century saw the birth of the man-made fibre industry, the culmination of the age-old drive to synthesize the mechanical and aesthetic properties of cocoon silk. Today, our sights are not set only on spider silk: we are also seeking alternative methods of producing polymers that are more akin to biology than heavy industry. This combination has inspired a new breed of entrepreneur. Today's pioneers are synthetic biologists and bio-engineers – a far cry from the early industrialists – seeking out ways to shift the paradigm of textile fibre production.

Biotechnology may sound like a new discipline, but its roots are steeped in centuries of processing technology for food; cultured goods, such as beer, wine, yoghurt, cheese and bread, use microorganisms to transform material (usually sugars) from one state into another in ambient conditions. Today, these microorganisms can be specially selected or engineered to carry out very specific tasks, such as clearing up contaminated sites or producing medicines.

RIGHT AND BELOW Details from the wet-
spinning production of filament fibres, the
process used by Bolt Threads to turn their
liquid protein into fibre.

FIBRES FROM
FERMENTATION

Bolt Threads is a young American company that
was set up by Dan Widmaier, David Breslauer
and Ethan Mirsky, a team of graduates who set
out to develop a commercial process that would
allow the production of engineered silk fibres
using fermentation. The technology emerged
from the study of spider silk and specifically the
relationship between fibre properties and DNA.
The findings informed the development of a
novel fermentation process able to grow protein
material with the same molecular structure as
spider silk using a soup of sugar, water, salt and
yeast. Genetically modified microorganisms are
used to consume the sugar and convert it into
liquid protein. The liquid protein is harvested,
processed and extruded into fibres using wet
spinning, a method that involves squeezing the
liquid through tiny holes into a bath of specialist
chemicals that solidify the liquid into fibres, a
process used to produce acrylic and rayon fibres.
Bolt Threads fibres are at pre-commercial stage
and the company plans to launch commercial
products including apparel in the near future.

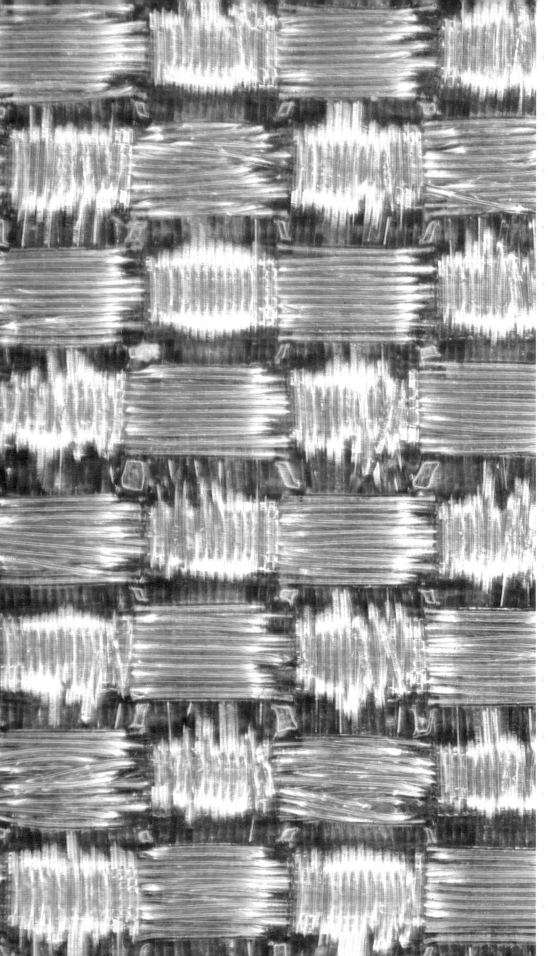

Microscopic view of woven textile made from filament yarns.

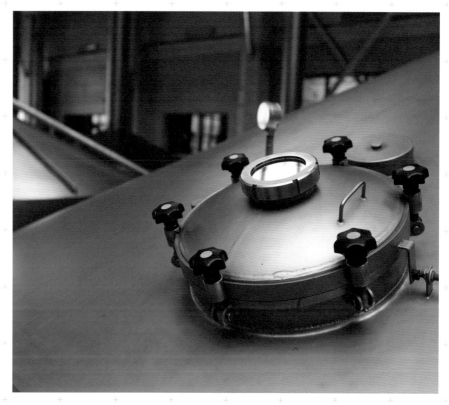

RIGHT Detail of the manhole of an industrial fermentation vat.

BELOW Industrial loom used for the production of woven textiles.

BACTERIAL CELLULOSE

Fermenting tea

BIOCOUTURE

Grown garment concept

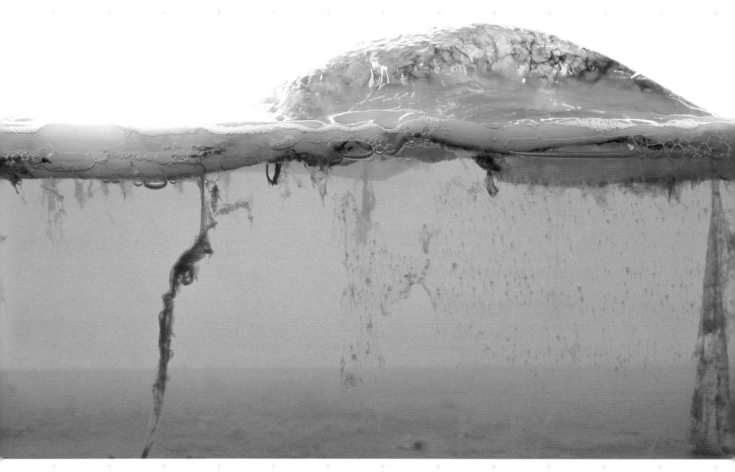

ABOVE Modified kombucha during fermentation, showing the cellulose skin forming on the surface of the liquid.

RIGHT Fermenting SCOBY culture floating on the surface.

Kombucha is an ancient beverage believed to have healing and health properties. It is produced by the fermentation of sweetened tea using a 'symbiotic colony of bacteria and yeast' (SCOBY) that has the appearance and texture of a thick rubbery wet skin. Although claims for its health benefits are not based on scientific evidence, the beverage contains vitamins C and B and organic acids (such as acids and enzymes) created by the culture as it digests the sugar.

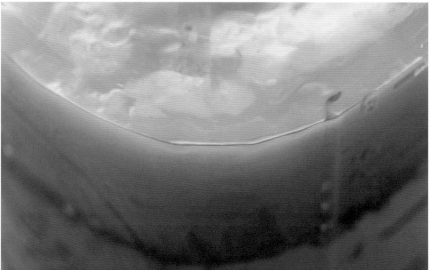

Biocouture kimono (right) and bomber jacket (below) made from dried sheets of bacterial cellulose with printed detail, and 'denim' jacket (bottom) made from bacterial cellulose dyed dark blue.

GROWN MATERIALS

There is a growing desire from the creative sectors to seek out and explore novel materials and methods of making things. Suzanne Lee, who originally trained as a fashion designer, has pioneered biofabrication (the creation of complex living and non-living products from biological systems such as living cells, bacteria and biochemical molecules) for the fashion and luxury industries. Her vision of microbes as the factories of the future drove Lee to explore ways of *growing* materials for apparel as an alternative to current practice. Lee set up Biocouture as a consultancy to explore the scope for grown materials in the fashion sector. Biocouture created a platform that enabled her to collaborate with biologists and experiment with fermentation.

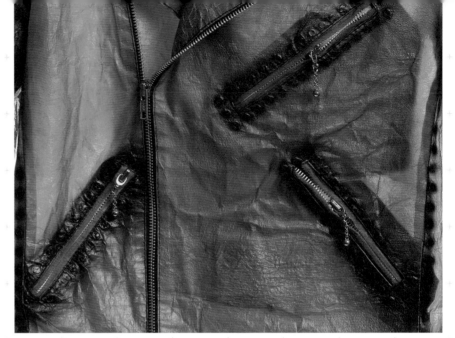

Lee became interested in the properties of SCOBY. The culture itself, made from long chains of cellulose microfibrils (clusters of cellulose polymers), has the ability to grow during fermentation and form sheets; when dried it creates a type of leathery material. Lee wanted to develop ways in which she could use these sheets of bacterial cellulose as a material for the production of garments. Following an intense experimental stage, she developed a unique 'tool box' and pioneered techniques that enabled her to manipulate colour, texture and shape to form experimental garments and accessories. This process has been adopted by numerous biohackers (non-institutional individuals experimenting with synthetic biology in makeshift labs) internationally, though it is still at an experimental stage. Developments in synthetic biology that will enable the tuning of the cellulose structure are necessary if this is to become a true alternative source of raw material, but it has strong potential as a platform for the biomimetic creation of information-rich materials (polymers whose properties are determined by the structural organization of monomers).

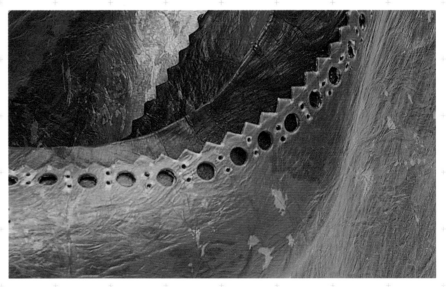

TOP Zip details from Biocouture's bacterial cellulose biker jacket.

CENTRE Rows of fermenting vats for growing bacterial cellulose material.

RIGHT Detail of Biocouture shoe made from bacterial cellulose material.

Biocouture bacterial cellulose shoe.

MYCELIUM

Nature's decomposer

MUSHROOM MATERIALS

Grown products

Mycelium forming in soil, showing the complex networks of fine roots called hyphae.

Fungi constitute a unique kingdom separate from that of animals, plants, bacteria and protists (whose members include single-cell organisms such as yeasts and moulds and multicellular organisms such as fruit-forming mushrooms). Fungi are heterotrophs – meaning that they can absorb food only in the form of broken-down polymers. Fungi play a critical role in the terrestrial and aquatic environments they inhabit because of their ability to decompose plant matter such as dead leaves and wood into nutrients, releasing essential raw materials back into the ecosystem. This process is executed through a complex root system known as mycelium. The fine roots called hyphae resemble a branching mass of fine thread-like filaments: these secrete specialized enzymes tasked with the breakdown of biological polymers such as cellulose into monomers.

MUSHROOM PACKAGING

Ecovative (**eco**logy inno**vative**) is a visionary US-based company that uses agricultural waste including stalks and seed husks to manufacture fully formed products as an alternative to thermoplastic polymers such as polystyrene, used extensively in packaging. The founders, Eben Bayer and Gavin McIntyre, discovered that the root-like filaments produced by mycelium during the digestion of agricultural waste function like a self-assembling polymer that binds mushroom and organic matter into a solid structure. This mushroom material demonstrates similar properties to plastic but is manufactured in ambient conditions, without the use of chemicals, and is completely compostable.

The first products to market made from Mushroom Materials were custom-moulded components used in the type of protective packaging that is normally made from polystyrene. Many ecologically conscious manufacturers have replaced polystyrene packaging with packaging made from Ecovative's material, and it is used to ship products ranging from sensitive electronics to heavy furniture. The company has grown significantly over the last few years and now employs a design team dedicated to creating a portfolio of products made from Mushroom Materials.

BELOW Brown beech mushroom, an edible mushroom native to East Asia.

BOTTOM Ecovative Mushroom Materials packaging products.

TISSUE CULTURES
Harvesting from living cells

MEAT AND MATERIALS
Victimless leather

Silk suture thread embedded with cells (inset: 40x magnification) in Amy Congdon's 'Tissue Engineered Textiles' experiment. The cells are highlighted using fluorescent microscopy.

Biofabrication can be defined as the production of complex living and non-living biological products from raw materials such as living cells, molecules, extracellular matrices, and biomaterials.

Vladimir Mironov, 2009

Originally the focus of the bioengineering discipline was on medical applications, for example attempting to grow tissue or organs for transplants to provide safer and more efficient procedures that did not rely on donors. Today, tissue engineering has more wide-reaching applications; techniques such as biofabrication have found relevance in the creation of novel materials for the food, cosmetics and even fashion industries.

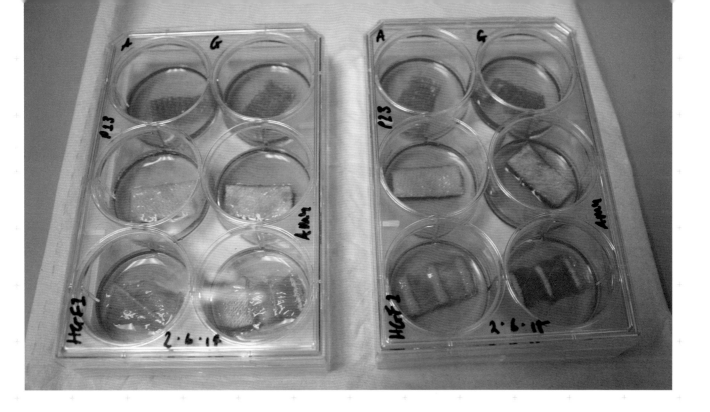

MODERN MEADOW

US-based Modern Meadow was founded in 2011 by Andras Forgacs, Gabor Forgacs, Francoise Marga and Karoly Jakab. This innovative company was concerned by the environmental impact of factory farming and the meat industry on a global scale coupled with the projected increase in demand from a growing world population and new emerging economies. The original team developed the idea of growing meat in a lab using technology that cultures cells from animals rather than slaughtering them. This novel process begins with small amounts of muscle or skin cells, obtained from the animal without harming it. These cells are nurtured in a clinical environment where they are left to grow and divide naturally. The team uses a tissue-engineering technique called biofabrication to grow leather from skin cells and meat from muscle in trays in a lab. Steak Chips, a biofabricated beef snack, was one of the company's early prototypes that earned it attention in the media.

Biofabricated leather from skin cells is a hugely important development for the fashion and consumer goods industries. The material itself is free from imperfections such as bites, scars and uneven colouring and can be grown to specific dimensions, keeping waste to a minimum. This victimless approach is at pre-commercial stages and if successful could deliver a significant paradigm shift to the traditional leather goods industry by significantly reducing environmental and ethical impact.

TOP Amy Congdon's scaffolds in culture.

ABOVE Leather drinking vessel. Animal hides have been used for the production of drinking vessels since the Neolithic period.

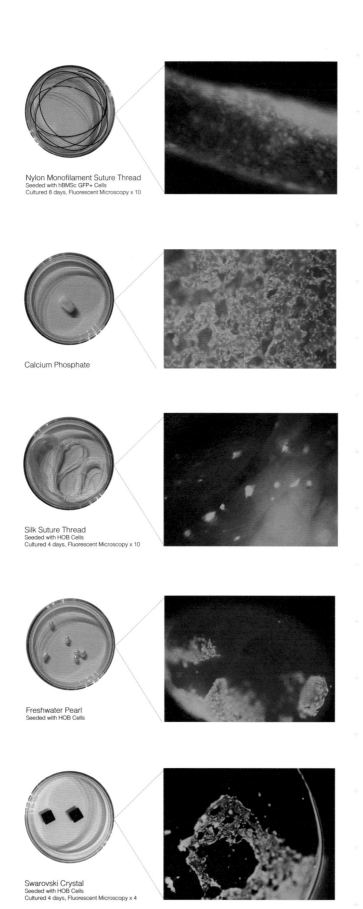

Nylon Monofilament Suture Thread
Seeded with hBMSc GFP+ Cells
Cultured 8 days, Fluorescent Microscopy x 10

Calcium Phosphate

Silk Suture Thread
Seeded with HOB Cells
Cultured 4 days, Fluorescent Microscopy x 10

Freshwater Pearl
Seeded with HOB Cells

Swarovski Crystal
Seeded with HOB Cells
Cultured 4 days, Fluorescent Microscopy x 4

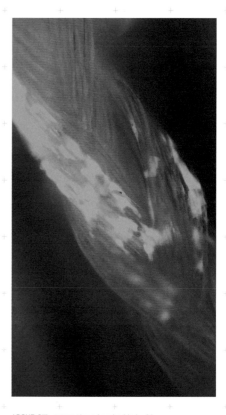

ABOVE Silk suture thread embedded with cells in Amy Congdon's research project.

LEFT Amy Congdon material experiments.

TISSUE ENGINEERED TEXTILES

Amy Congdon is a London-based designer interested in exploring the crossovers between design and science, and in particular using tissue cultures to create materials for fashion and jewelry. Congdon swapped the traditional design studio for the life science laboratories at King's College London to further her research and understanding of the current capabilities of these technologies. 'Tissue Engineered Textiles' is an ongoing research project in collaboration with Professor Lucy Di-Silvio, Professor of Tissue Engineering at King's College London, looking at how textile techniques can inform new approaches to growing our future materials and products by culturing cells over specially designed digitally embroidered scaffolds and experimenting with cell growth. Although at an experimental stage, Congdon's work could lead to a completely new class of biodegradable material for product and fashion design that is *grown* in ambient conditions, using natural processes.

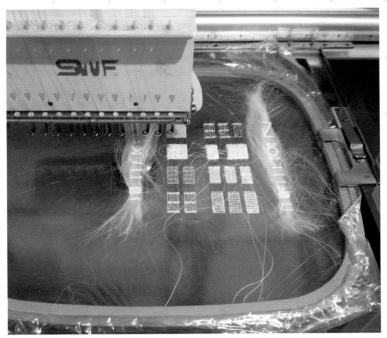

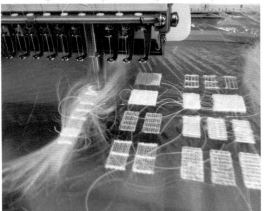

TOP Jars used to sterilize scaffolds for
Amy Congdon's Tissue Engineered Textiles.

LEFT AND ABOVE Images of Amy Congdon's
textile scaffolds being created using a
commercial digital embroidery machine.

PHOTOSYNTHESIS

From carbon dioxide to sugar and oxygen

BIOBATTERIES

Plant-inspired alternative energy

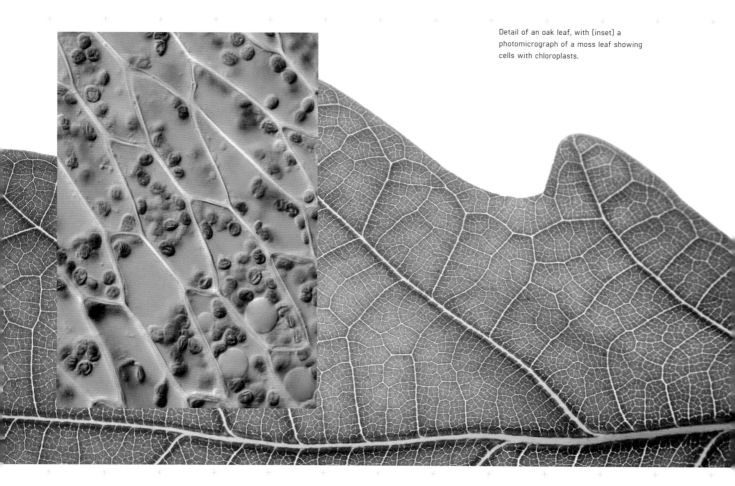

Detail of an oak leaf, with (inset) a photomicrograph of a moss leaf showing cells with chloroplasts.

Global forests annually remove 2.4 billion tons of carbon and absorb 8.8 billion tons of carbon dioxide from the atmosphere.

US Forest Service, 2011

Trees are truly remarkable organisms inextricably linked with all life on Earth. Living organisms produce carbon dioxide, which trees absorb, in return releasing the oxygen necessary for sustaining life. Since industrialization, forests have functioned as a carbon dioxide sink, cleaning pollution, in the form of carbon dioxide, from the air and converting it into glucose.

The air-filtering function happens through the leaves, which contain a molecule called chlorophyll (also responsible for the green colour). Through a series of reactions known as

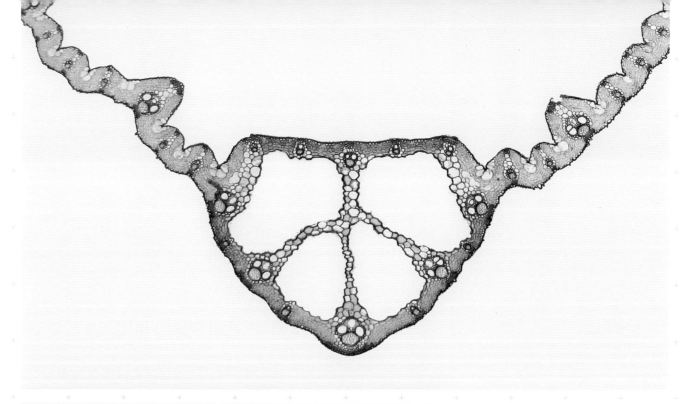

ABOVE A cross-section of a rice leaf
at 40x magnification.

LEFT Detail of a fern leaf.

photosynthesis, chlorophyll uses the energy in
sunlight to convert water and carbon dioxide
into glucose and oxygen (gas released into the
atmosphere). During photosynthesis light energy
from the sun is converted into chemical energy
through the production of glucose molecules.
Glucose molecules are used for respiration (gas
exchange in plants) or stored in the form of starch.
Trees function effectively as an enormous battery
able to capture and store some of the sun's
energy: living organisms store less than 0.1 per
cent of the sun's energy reaching the Earth, and
50 per cent of that energy is stored in trees.

The sun represents a greatly underused
sustainable source of energy; photovoltaic solar cell
technology to convert solar energy into electricity
is improving, but these devices are a long way
from becoming part of our everyday lives. One of
the key barriers is that the materials used for their
production require high-energy processes. By
contrast, leaves grow in ambient conditions.

ABOVE Silicon wafers are used in electronics for the fabrication of integrated circuits and in photovoltaics for conventional, wafer-based solar cells.

BELOW Silicon crystal with photovoltaic cells.

BIOBATTERIES

In 2010, a pioneering team of scientists led by Professor Won Hyoung Ryu from Yansei University in South Korea and Stanford University, California, succeeded in generating electrical current from the electron activity in individual algae cells during photosynthesis. The team developed a technique that allowed them to extract a tiny electrical current by inserting ultra-sharp nano-electrodes made of gold into the chloroplasts (photosynthesizing organs) of algal cells. This promising breakthrough could be a first step towards generating high-efficiency bioelectricity that does not give off carbon dioxide as a byproduct. Ryu's team were able to harvest just one picoampere (a millionth of a millionth of an ampere) of electricity from a single cell; in reality it would take a trillion cells photosynthesizing for one hour to equal the amount of energy stored in an AA battery. Furthermore, the cells die after an hour (possibly because starved of energy), so much work remains to be done. Harvesting bioelectricity would be significantly more efficient and sustainable than burning biofuels. Ryu estimates his process is about 20 per cent efficient (conventional photovoltaic cells are currently about 20–40 per cent efficient), and he hopes to reach 100 per cent efficiency in the near future.

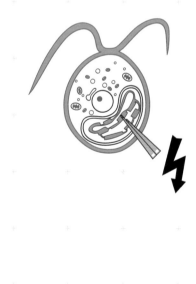

LATRO LAMP

Designer Mark Thompson of Eindhoven, the Netherlands, envisions a future inspired by Ryu's work where electrical devices are powered by bioelectricity harvested from algae during photosynthesis. Latro (Latin for 'thief') is a design concept exploring this potential future market.

Technological advances at nano scale have paved the way for the development of energy-efficient components for electrical devices such as LEDs. Thompson's Latro lamp combines the energy potential of algae with the functionality of a hanging lamp. The algae reside in the upper section of the lamp and the owner is required to breathe into the device's handle to introduce carbon dioxide, necessary for photosynthesis. The lamp must then be placed in sunlight for photosynthesis to commence. As carbon dioxide and water undergo conversion, oxygen is released through the spout. Light intensity is monitored by a sensor that allows electron harvesting when excitation levels pass a certain threshold, so that bioelectricity can be harvested without leaving the algae malnourished. Energy generated can be stored in a battery for use as required.

The Latro lamp prototype. Energy produced by the algae is used to generate light.

ABOVE AND RIGHT Illustration of the Latro lamp concept.

BOTTOM RIGHT Schematic diagram showing how energy from the algae is harvested, stored in a battery, and used to power a light.

Our future energy needs will be met by various sources, not least by tapping into the energy capacity of our most immediate, natural surroundings.

Mark Thompson

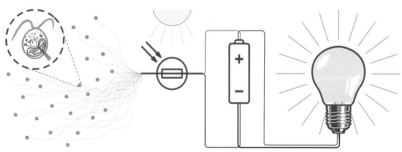

BACTERIA

Microbial factories

HYBRID ELECTRONICS

Intersection of biology and machine

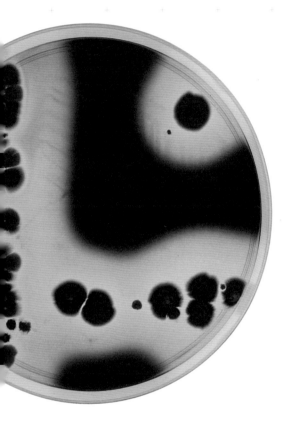
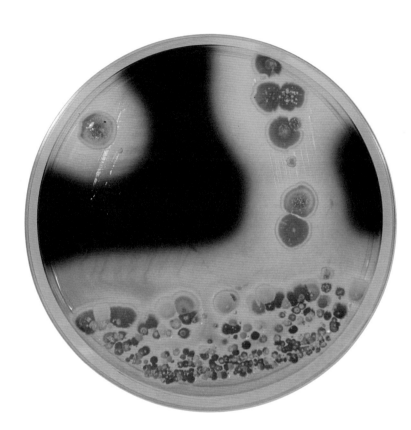

Actinomycete bacteria growing on agar.

Microorganisms such as bacteria, fungi and yeasts are capable of forming incredibly complex communities enclosed from the outside environment in a complex polymeric substance produced by the organisms, which functions both as a protective barrier that allows the organism to survive in hostile environments and as a way of storing nutrients, water and other local resources. These microscopic cooperatives are called biofilms and are very common in the natural world. Bacterial biofilms function in a coordinated manner and are capable of self-assembly, resource management and many other behaviours more akin to multicellular beings than single-cell microorganisms. The sophisticated nature of biofilms, especially bacterial biofilms,

represents great opportunities for synthetic biologists because they can use science to control the formation and behaviour of such communities as a way of engineering a new breed of bio-hybrid materials and devices.

BACTERIAL ELECTRONICS

In 2003, an interdisciplinary team of scientists and engineers from Harvard University and Massachusetts Institute of Technology (MIT), led by Allen Chen and Timothy Lu, developed the capability to manipulate gene networks to create a new class of living materials that contain non-living components such as gold nanoparticles and quantum dots (nano-scale crystals of

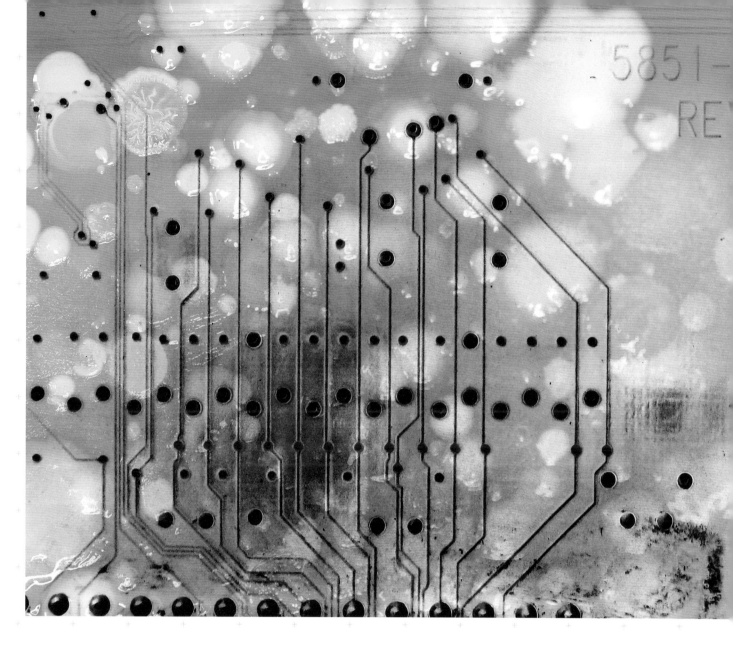

A concept image of a bio-electronic circuit.

semiconducting material). Modified bacterial cells have been designed to produce biofilms that can host non-living components. These hybrid living systems can do things typical of living organisms, such as self-assemble and self-heal, in addition to things typical of non-living systems, such as emit light and conduct electrical current.

The team uses the bacterium *Escherichia coli* because it naturally produces biofilms containing 'curli' fibres – hairlike structures that enable the *E. coli* bacterium to attach to various surfaces. The curli fibres are made from a repeating chain of a type of protein subunit. Lu and his colleagues have developed a method of modifying the curli fibre structure by introducing peptides, which enable the capture of non-living nanoparticles such as gold, tiny crystals or quantum dots, and incorporating them into the biofilm.

This extends the reach of synthetic biology into very specific electronic and optical device production. The team envisions applications ranging from batteries and solar cells to biofuels and diagnostic devices. In the future, bacteria could manufacture components and indeed entire electrical devices.

SLIME MOULD

Master logic

BRAINLESS COMPUTING

Amoeba processors

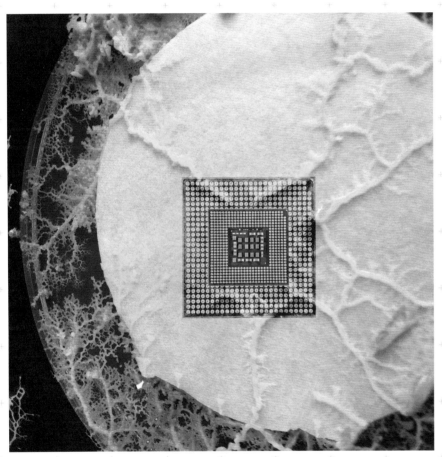

ABOVE A concept image of a bio-processing device.

ABOVE RIGHT Slime mould moves over a surface like a giant amoeba ingesting organic matter.

Slime moulds are simple organisms capable of incredibly complex behaviours. *Physarum polycephalum*, or 'many-headed slime', is not actually a mould: it is a type of single-cell amoeba without a brain or nervous system. *P. polycephalum* is a soil-dwelling organism usually found on forest floors, where individual cells club together to rummage through leaf litter and logs looking for bacteria, fungal spores and other microbes, which it envelops and digests.

Colonies of individual *P. polycephalum* form foraging networks of tubes, or tendrils, that branch out to transport nutrients from one point to another. Researchers studying this behaviour discovered that this collective of brainless organisms was capable of making some very

complicated decisions. Experiments conducted in the controlled environment of a lab using cells confined to a petri dish revealed that the slime mould network was able to identify the quickest route to food by navigating complex landscapes such as a maze simply by spreading out to fill the entire system: tendrils that did not find a food source retracted, leaving behind a trail of slime that informed other cells that this particular location was of no interest and thus should be avoided while resources were focused on fruitful pathways.

The next step was to test the scope of this logic. Scientists designed experiments that involved arranging items of food in the positions of major cities and urban areas. Astonishingly, the *P. polycephalum* colony recreated, in miniature, the rail system of Tokyo and the major roadways of Canada, Britain, Portugal and Spain with uncanny accuracy. The *P. polycephalum* was able to solve, in just twenty-six hours, real-world problems that took teams of urban planners, engineers and architects decades to work out.

SLIME-MOULD COMPUTING

Andrew Adamatzky, Professor of Unconventional Computing at the University of West England, and Theresa Schubert, a post-media artist at Bauhaus-University Weimar, Germany, believe the properties of *P. polycephalum* could bring about a paradigm shift in computer science – from silicon to bio-computing. These single-cell organisms could function as a logical circuit and thus form the building blocks of living computers. In their experimental work the cross-disciplinary team found that they could manipulate the organism to mechanically activate 'gates' that open and shut, like the logic gates of computer chips, blocking and redirecting the flow of fragments. The team showed that the '*P. polycephalum* network' could carry out simple functions of Boolean logic, a key system in binary computing. The potential for this technology is the creation of cheap, disposable, self-growing and self-repairing 'wetware'.

SLIME-MOULD-CONTROLLED ROBOT

Dr Klaus-Peter Zauner from Southampton University is an engineer who has created a robot controlled by a type of slime mould. Zauner grew a star-shaped sample of a specific form of *P. polycephalum* that naturally dislikes light and attached each of its six points to a leg of a six-legged robot. He was able to control the movement of the robot by shining white light on to a section of the organism that made it vibrate and change its thickness. These vibrations were transmitted to a computer, which then sent signals to move the leg in question. Zauner found that pointing beams of light at different parts of the slime mould encouraged the movement of different legs, and was eventually able to make the robot walk. Zauner imagines a future where robotic devices will be controlled by living organisms able to self-repair and self-restructure.

05

BIOLOGY

TOWARDS 4D DESIGN

BIOMIMETIC APPLICATION

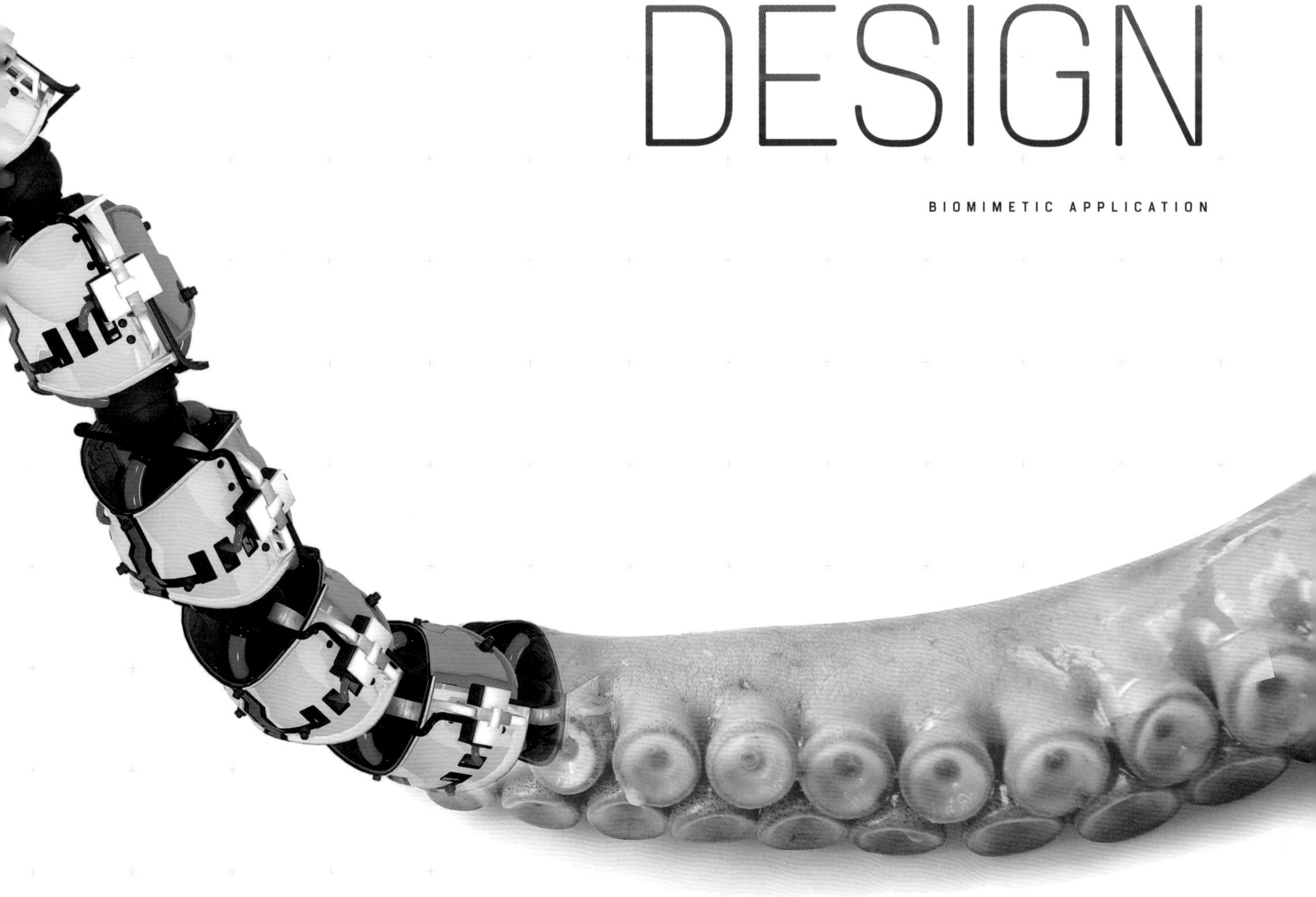

From scratches on cave walls to the digital revolution, the nature of information generation, storage and management has altered dramatically. Today, data is a commodity that can be exchanged, stored and mined using digital technologies deeply embedded in modern life. The nature of information in biology has not altered; temperature, moisture, chemicals (such as scent) and light are all carriers of information. The previous chapter, Making, initiated an exploration into physical forms of information in biological systems and how they can inspire the creation of low-energy, sustainable, closed-loop products. Work initiated by synthetic biology groups has begun to explore a shift towards information-rich materials and structures that could enable us to do more with less in a way that does not trap resources or draw on depleting energy supplies.

This chapter will explore ways of introducing information to man-made structures to enable advanced, *life-like* behaviours such as logic, self-assembly, self-repair and autonomous motion without circuitry, motors and electricity: in other words, towards **4D design** – in which both spatial and temporal elements are encompassed, so that the qualities of properties of an object alter in relation to stimuli at some future point. This field of **programmable** materials and structures is in its infancy, yet small steps, mostly conducted in labs and experimental studios, begin to reveal a world where the nature of things is very different.

SQUID NERVES | SCHMITT TRIGGER

Cell conductivity | Analogue to digital conversion

Detail of a swimming squid. For the invention of what he originally called a 'thermionic trigger', Otto Schmitt was inspired by his study of the nerve impulses of squid.

Otto Schmitt, the father of modern biomimetics (see p.10), was a prolific innovator in the fields of electrical engineering, biophysics and bioengineering. With undergraduate and postgraduate degrees in zoology, physics and mathematics, Schmitt had a unique perspective on natural phenomena. Described as an individual of inordinate curiosity, Schmitt at one point gained inspiration from watching frogs, spending hours observing the creatures in order to solve some of the challenges he encountered in electrical engineering. Wanting to understand the decision-making process frogs used to distinguish which lily pad to leap to, after hours of observation he deduced that the frog continuously logged its position by sending feedback to its muscles and made its leap when the perfect trajectory was identified. He applied this idea to the development of self-adjusting electronic circuits.

Schmitt was professor of biophysics, bioengineering and electrical engineering at the University of Minnesota from 1949 until 1983, where he founded the university's Biophysics

Lab. During his career he developed many of the fundamental electronic components that drive our devices today, such as emitter followers and differential amplifiers as used in numerous applications from industrial controls to amplifiers and audio-video systems.

Schmitt developed the invention that bears his name in 1938 as part of his doctorate work, during which he studied the conductivity of squid nerves and the way in which electrical impulses transmit from one nerve cell to another. Schmitt applied this information to the design of an electronic circuit that enables a constant electronic signal to instigate an on/off state. The circuit is called a 'trigger' because the output retains its value until a sufficient alteration in input value triggers a change. The Schmitt trigger is used to convert analogue into digital signals and has countless electronic applications, including in computer keyboards.

RIGHT The European squid.

BELOW Detail of an electronic circuit board.

BOTTOM Part of an old printed circuit board with electronic components.

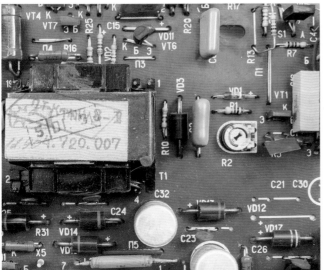

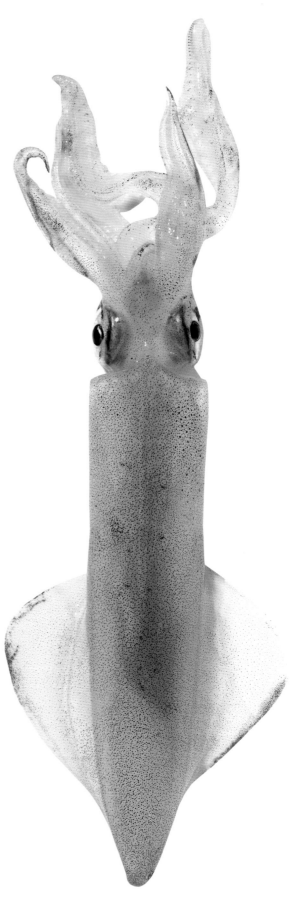

ARTIFICIAL INTELLIGENCE

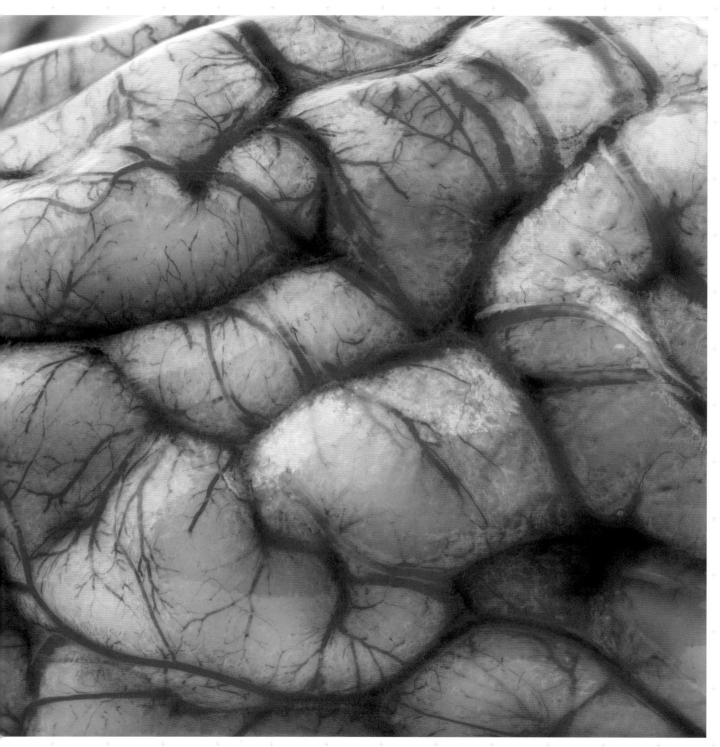

BIOMIMETIC APPLICATION

INTELLIGENT MACHINES

Synthetic minds

Artificial Intelligence – the science and engineering of making intelligent machines.

John McCarthy, 1955

OPPOSITE Detail of sheep brain.

ABOVE The AIBO Robotic pet developed by Sony.

Tales of synthetic, autonomous beings date back millennia; this type of primeval science fiction is common to several ancient cultures. The ancient Greek myth of Talos describes a giant bronze humanoid robot that protected the noble Phoenican woman Europa from kidnappers and invaders on Crete by circling the island coast three times a day. Modern fiction is also populated by such characters; Mary Shelley's Gothic classic *Frankenstein* (1818) tells of a humanoid creature made of reclaimed body parts scavenged from the recently deceased, while science fiction author Philip K. Dick describes biorobotic beings that appear identical to humans in *Do Androids Dream of Electric Sheep?* (1968). Both these narratives describe the trials and tribulations of artificial living beings, underpinned by the ethical concerns of humans surrounding the field of artificial intelligence.

The field of AI research was founded in the summer of 1956 as a result of a research project organized by the American computer scientist John McCarthy in partnership with Marvin Minsky, Allen Newell, Arthur Samuel, and Herbert Simon (who became leaders in the field) at Dartmouth College in Hanover, New Hampshire. The impact of early work conducted in this area is not obvious to the average consumer; however, behind the scenes it has supported significant leaps in sectors such as medical diagnostics and data mining. Intelligent personal assistants in smartphones, such as Siri (Apple), Cortana (Microsoft) and Google Now, use algorithms based on early AI research, as does the Kinect 3D body-motion interface for the Xbox 360 and Xbox One.

ROBOTIC PET

AIBO (**A**rtificial **I**ntelligence Ro**BO**t), the world's first robotic pet, emerged from the collaboration between engineer Toshitada Doi and artificial intelligence expert Masahiro Fujita at Sony's Computer Science Laboratory (CSL), and was launched in 1999. Doi enlisted the help of erotic illustrator Hajime Sorayama, whose subject-matter focused on cyborg/feminine robot themes, to create the initial designs for AIBO's body. AIBO is a Japanese homonym for friend, pal or sidekick; the robot's popular form was a doglike structure. Its specifications evolved over several generations, with the final model featuring voice recognition, pressure sensors on paws and chin, and electric static sensors on the back and head; its eyes were linked to a sophisticated camera and an LED display capable of demonstrating more than sixty emotional states. This advanced technical system enabled the robot to interact with its owners in a complex and intimate fashion. Although AIBO was discontinued in 2006, the product marked a significant milestone in the history of design, and examples of the 'entertainment robot' are part of the permanent collections of the Museum of Modern Art (MoMA) in New York and the Smithsonian Institution in Washington, DC.

SYNTHETIC BRAIN

The human brain is an immensely powerful, energy-efficient, self-learning, self-repairing computer. Researchers at the cutting edge of AI today believe that if we could understand and mimic the way it works, we could apply it to technologies that would revolutionize computing, medicine and society.

The Blue Brain Project began in 2005 as a small consortium of European partners. The aim was to reconstruct the brain piece by piece and build a virtual brain in a supercomputer to provide a tool for neuroscientists to obtain a better understanding of neurological diseases.

Within five years the team, led by Henry Markram, a professor at the École Polytechnique Fédérale de Lausanne in Switzerland, had successfully simulated the rat cortical column, a (compared to human) simple neuronal network the size of a pinhead. The resulting tool was able to create realistic models of the brain's essential building blocks. The models produced by Blue Brain correlated with years of previous neuroscientific observations and experiments.

Based on the success of the Blue Brain Project, the consortium grew significantly (from thirteen partners to eighty-six), forming a European supergroup dedicated to the creation of a virtual human brain that became the Human Brain Project (HBP).

Markram, director of the HBP, believes that the knowledge gained from modelling the human brain will allow us to design supercomputers, robots, sensors and other devices with superior intelligence to what is currently possible. The work will help us to understand the root causes of brain diseases, allowing early diagnosis and the development of new treatments while reducing reliance on animal testing. The group also plans to explore questions of a more philosophical nature such as what it means to perceive, to think, to remember, to learn, to know and to make decisions.

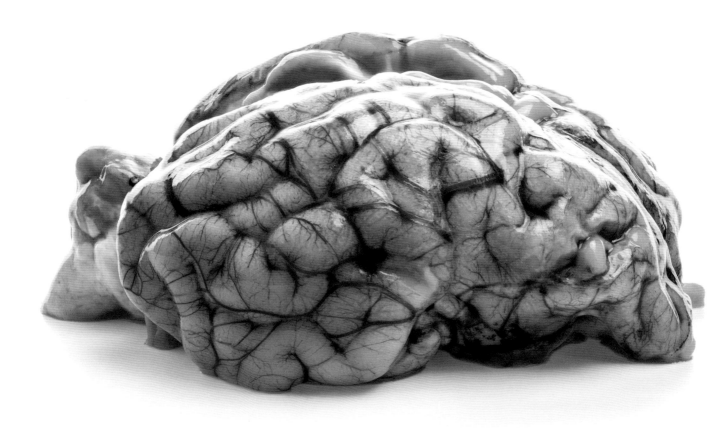

ABOVE Astrocytes are characteristic
star-shaped cells found in the cerebral
cortex (as here) and the spinal cord.

OPPOSITE A sheep brain.

THOUGHT IN A LAB

Creating models of the brain is a vital method
of studying the way this organ works. Instead of
using supercomputers, a team of neuroscientists
led by Professor Michael Coleman at Aston
University in the UK has developed a novel way
to model workings of the human brain and
create the basics of synthetic thought. Working
with modified tumour cells that have been
programmed to stop multiplying, the team
uses a natural molecule employed by the
body to stimulate cellular development to turn
the cells into a co-culture of nerve and astrocyte
cells – basic components of the brain. These
co-cultures are developed into minuscule
connected cell balls known as neurospheres.
Neurospheres are capable of processing
information at a simple level, which essentially
forms the basis of thought. The team's ambition
is to use these microscopic cell clusters to
develop new treatments for debilitating
neurodegenerative diseases including
Alzheimer's, motor neurone and Parkinson's.

SWARM INTELLIGENCE

ABOVE Young or half-grown barracudas
may group together in schools.

RIGHT Huge flocks of starlings are often
seen wheeling through the sky at dusk.

Animals living in organized societies that extend
beyond a simple family group are common
in nature. Colonies of bees, ants or termites,
schools of fish and flocks of birds are all examples
of 'swarm societies'. These flocks, schools
and swarms of living organisms demonstrate
sophisticated leaderless cooperative behaviours
that have intrigued researchers from biology,
mathematics and robotics for several decades –
a fascination that has led to the emergence of the
new discipline of 'swarm intelligence' (SI). Swarm
intelligence focuses on the collective behaviour of
decentralized, self-organized natural or artificial
systems that results from the local interactions of
individuals with each other and the environment.

FIRE ANTS | SWARM ROBOTICS

Collaborative superorganism | Self-assembly systems

The cooperative behaviour of ants is a well-known phenomenon; these tiny insects work together to complete complex tasks involving foraging, building nests and cultivating food. Nathan Mlot, a graduate student in mechanical engineering at Georgia Institute of Technology, USA, wanted to understand why single fire ants (*Solenopsis invicta*) strugglc in water, yet as a group they can float effortlessly for months.

    S. invicta originates in the rainforests in Brazil, which are subject to regular heavy flooding. In order to survive in this habitat, the fire ants have evolved ingenious strategies to maintain coherence within their colonies. Mlot used time-lapse photography to capture the mechanism behind these extraordinary behaviours. The results of this work revealed that the ants self-assemble to create structures that function as ladders, chains, walls and rafts, composed exclusively of individual ants linked together by their mandibles and legs. Fire ant rafts are long-lasting structures that enable an entire colony to keep together and float for months if necessary, seeking new territories to inhabit. A novel set of properties emerges from the ant collective: the raft is water-repellent, incredibly robust and capable of self-healing. These qualities suggest that when fire ants join forces as a collective they become a superorganism.

Fire ants working together.

The swarm of Kilobots developed at Harvard University. Each is just over 3 cm (1.25 in) high.

SWARM ROBOTICS

Research groups study the behaviour of biological examples such as ant colonies, bird flocks, animal herds, schools of fish, bacterial growth and so on to understand the nature of communication in what appears to be random interaction between individuals and how that influences the emergence of intelligent collective behaviour. The resulting 'swarm principles' are translated into algorithms and fed into computers. These algorithms are often used to create models for simulations and to make predictions, and are applied to experimental populations of simple robots.

SI has given rise to the new discipline of swarm robotics, a novel approach to the coordination of multi-robot systems composed of large numbers of uncomplicated robots with a simple inbuilt constant feedback system such as radio frequency or infrared. The hypothesis is that incredibly complex behaviours can emerge from interactions among simple robots or between the robots and their environment.

One of the initial focuses in the development of swarm robotic technology is the production of simple, cheap, disposable individual robots. The LIBOT Robotic System is an example of a super-low-cost swarm designed to operate outdoors; these robots use GPS and a transceiver module to communicate with each other and the base station.

The Colias microrobot, built in the Computer Intelligence Lab at the University of Lincoln, UK, features an obstacle-detection mechanism based on the visual system of the locust. These insects have evolved specialized neurons called 'lobula giant movement detectors' that react to objects directly approaching the insect's eyes, enabling the locust to take evasive action. Similarly, three short-range sensors coupled to a simple processor detect obstacles as they get closer to the individual robot. Communication with other members of the community is conducted through long-range infrared proximity sensors.

In 2014, Harvard University's Self-organizing Systems Research Group, led by Professor Radhika Nagpal, built the world's largest swarm of individual robots, called Kilobots. The Kilobot collective consists of 1,024 individual, simple, three-legged robotic devices each only a few centimetres across, which communicate via infrared and are capable of self-assembling into various formations such as a five-pointed starfish or letters of the alphabet.

In their current format, swarm robots are an essential research tool for studying swarm logic and improving the device design, but potential applications for this type of technology are numerous. Initial applications are in defence and space exploration (for example planetary mapping) as well as multipurpose self-assembly. Other potential applications include the development of nano-scale robots that can enter the body to locate and attack specific diseased sites such as cancer tumours.

TOP RIGHT Concept designs for miniature robots.

ABOVE Scenes from the *Skinsucka* concept exploring notions of human–robot symbiosis, showing a swarm of tiny microbots extruding a material web around the body (top), scavenging dead skin from the face (centre) and spinning a garment around the body (bottom).

SKINSUCKA

Skinsucka is a four-minute film, or 'design provocation', resulting from a collaboration between Clive van Heerden, Jack Mama and the creative director of fashion and technology firm Studio XO, Nancy Tilbury. The aim of *Skinsucka* is to critique hyper-consumerism and the exploitative forces of fast fashion that enable garments to be produced in developing countries, shipped to the West and retailed, all for less than the cost of 'junk food'. The film shows a fictional future scenario where microbial-powered swarm microbots share our living spaces and work behind the scenes performing a host of actions, such as scavenging household dirt and converting it into energy and material. The *Skinsucka* microbots extrude matter, like a 'swarm' of spiders, weaving garments directly around the body. Although the aim of the work is to challenge consumers to consider the ethical issues surrounding the products we consume, the sustainability of the resources used and the overall social and environmental impact of our current consumption behaviour, it also illustrates a potential future scenario where humans and robotic swarms live in symbiosis.

BIOROBOTICS

As imagined by modern science fiction writers, biots, replicants, Cylons and windups are all forms of advanced humanoid robots that look and behave just like human beings. In reality the field of biorobotics is by far the most active in biomimetics and explores a wide cross-section of biological examples from plants to animals, to develop systems capable of locomotion, flight and sensing, as well as bio-hybrid (man–machine) systems for rehabilitation.

'Biorobotics' is a term used to describe a subfield of robotics that specializes in the study of creating robots that emulate or simulate living biological organisms. The quest to develop robots that can overcome random obstacles and navigate hostile terrains has received heavy investment from space and defence agencies internationally. Multiple approaches are under investigation in labs across the globe; forms of locomotion from walking, jumping and crawling to swimming and flying are under development, predominantly in their technological infancy.

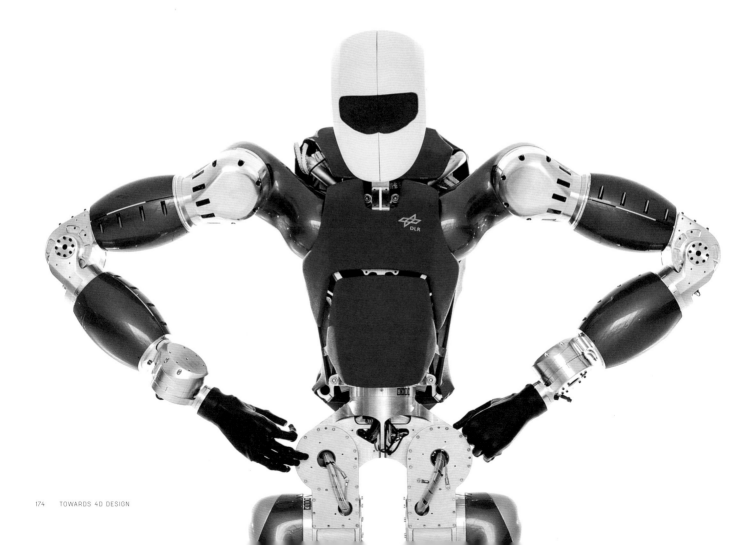

TORO THE HUMANOID ROBOT

TORO (TORque-controlled humanoid RObot) is a project initiated by the German Aerospace Centre (Deutsches Zentrum für Luft- und Raumfahrt, or DLR) to develop a walking machine. The robot has gone through several generations since work commenced in 2009. In its current format, TORO is complete with a head that houses a camera, together with a torso, arms and legs furnished with sophisticated sensors that aid it in learning how to perform simple actions that humans perform intuitively, such as opening a door or climbing steps.

TORO can mimic human walking biomechanics by moving forward in small but sturdy steps, smoothly, by setting one foot down in front of the other. The robot's designers have given it feet that are much smaller than other humanoid walking machines, which allow TORO to climb over obstacles with greater ease. The technology in the robot's arms and legs is based on existing knowledge in lightweight robotics as used, for example, in car manufacturing. The aim is to teach TORO how to operate independently in unknown environments, and to identify and develop further technologies that will eventually allow humanoid robots to venture into the unknown territories of space and carry out surveillance, repair or other necessary functions.

OPPOSITE DLR's torque-controlled humanoid robot, TORO. The robot has robust articulated prosthetic hands for interaction with the environment.

LEFT TORO weighs approximately 75 kg (165 lb) and is 1.6 m (63 in) tall.

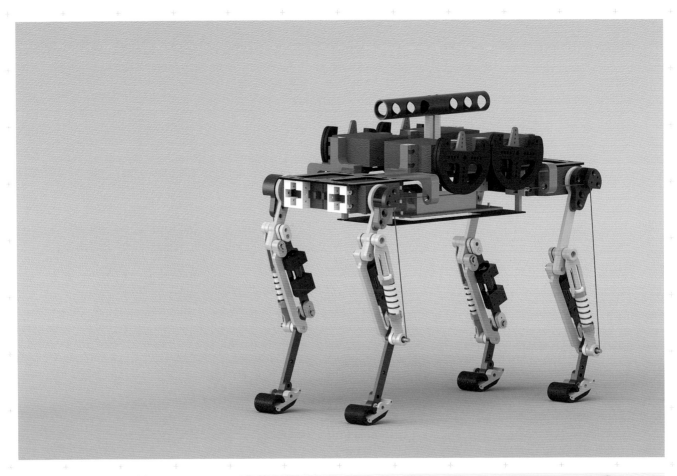

ABOVE AND RIGHT The Cheetah-cub has bio-inspired three-segment legs that use springs to approximate the muscle and tendon functions in animals.

CHEETAH-CUB

Four-legged robots that imitate the biomechanics of cats, dogs and even horses are an alternative approach that offers advantages in terms of speed and stability over their two-legged counterparts. The Cheetah-cub, for example, developed in the Biorobotics Laboratory at the École Polytechnique Fédérale de Lausanne in Switzerland, is an agile quadrupedal (four-legged) robot the size of a young cheetah cub or a domestic cat. The robot weighs 1 kilogram (2.2 pounds) and is approximately 21 centimetres (8 inches) long. Its leg design is based on the structure of the cheetah's leg, making it remarkably fast: it can reach speeds of 1.42 metres per second (3.2 miles per hour) – that is, about seven body lengths per second. This makes Cheetah-cub one of the fastest four-legged robots under 30 kilos (66 pounds). The robot is currently used as a research tool to further the state of the art in multi-segment legs in quadruped robots.

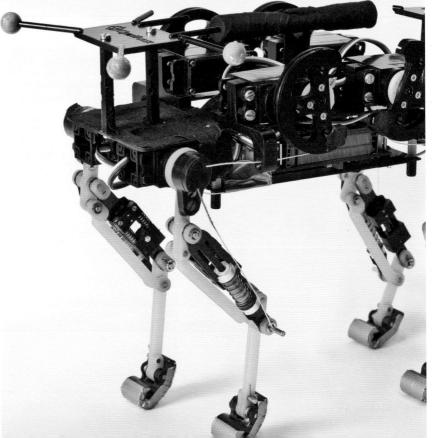

LEFT RoboBee is the world's smallest flying robot.

ABOVE An octocopter (eight-rotor) drone used for video and photographic productions.

BELOW A concept image showing how drones could be used to deliver goods purchased online.

ROBOBEE

Bees are among the most agile of flying insects, able to navigate from flower to flower effortlessly and hover stably while carrying relatively heavy loads. If microrobotic devices were able to emulate the physical robustness of bees and their ability to coordinate themselves in large numbers, the swarm of microrobots would be able to accomplish complex tasks faster, more efficiently and more reliably than the larger swarm robots. A team incorporating experts from Harvard's School of Engineering and Applied Sciences (SEAS), Harvard's Wyss Institute for Biologically Inspired Engineering, and microelectronics firm Centeye, has come together and created RoboBee, a microrobot whose design and functions are based on the biology and collective behaviour of the bee colony.

Professor Robert Wood, head of the Microrobotics Lab, is one of the key members of the RoboBee group, and achieved the world's first successful flight of a life-sized robotic fly in 2007. RoboBee is slightly larger than a penny yet can flap its wings 120 times a second and weighs only 80 milligrams. This technology has formed the basis of the RoboBee project. The team aims to develop the device to mimic the aerobatic behaviour of the bee and create a coordinated agile swarm of robotic insects with numerous, ubiquitous applications, such as crop pollination, search and rescue, exploration of extreme and hazardous environments, surveillance, and weather and climate mapping.

PLANT ROOTS

Advanced exploration and infiltration

PLANTOID

Smart anchor

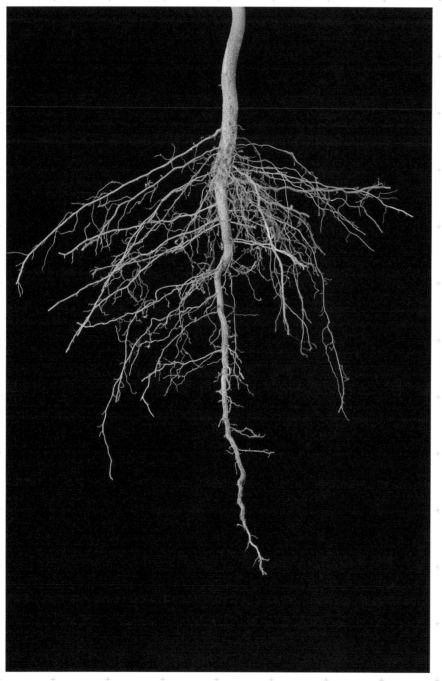

Plant roots demonstrate an amazing ability to explore unknown terrain, adapt to environmental pressures and penetrate the most complex structures. They achieve this through a combination of structural and behavioural elements; each plant deploys a growing network of branching roots armed with sophisticated sensing capabilities to explore the surrounding environment, seeking minerals and moisture to absorb. Barbara Mazzolai from the Center for Micro-BioRobotics at the Istituto Italiano di Tecnologia, near Pisa, Italy, coordinated the formation of a European consortium of materials and robotics specialists to create PLANTOID, a robotic system capable of demonstrating root-type behaviours in terms of advanced sensing, exploring and coordination capabilities that require minimal resources to operate.

A PLANTOID robotic system consists of an apex that houses sophisticated sensing, actuation and control units based on the design of the root tip. The apex is connected to the main robotic trunk via a soft, conformable, elongated root-type structure. In its current format the PLANTOID system functions as a research tool used to test biological hypotheses and models to improve understanding of root biomechanics. It also serves to fuel the development of further technologies that will enable this type of robot to identify a range of different applications such as space anchoring devices, exploration or construction tools, medical apparatus and consumer devices.

A tree root with its complex branching structure. Typically the root lies below the soil surface in vascular plants (plants that use a system of vessels, such as xylem, to move water and nutrients).

RIGHT Detail of the PLANTOID prototype featuring branches with smart leaf systems.

BELOW Detail of robotic root tip.

BELOW RIGHT The PLANTOID prototype. The robotic roots are designed to imitate the behaviour of plant roots with a particular focus on their penetrative, explorative and adaptive capacities.

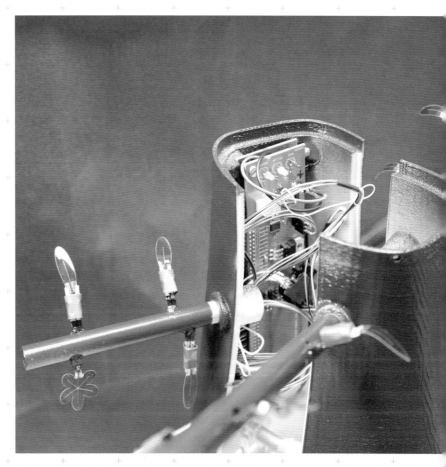

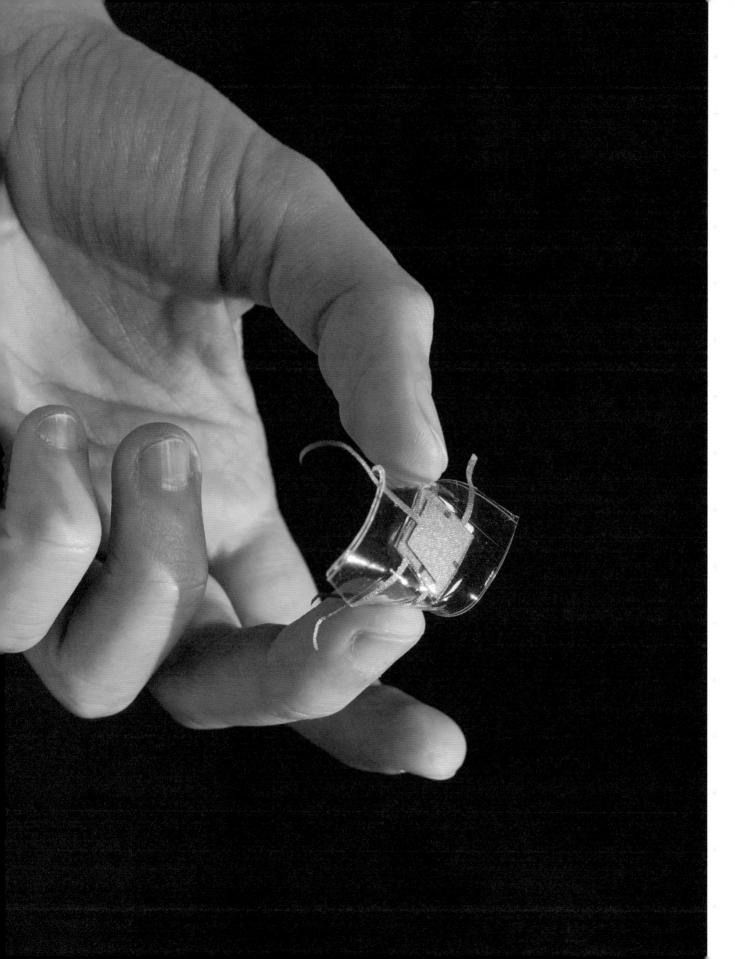

Components developed for the PLANTOID
prototype: smart soft component
(opposite), actuator (above) and specialist
actuator (right).

BIOLOGY

MAN–MACHINE
HYBRIDS

Bionic prosthetics

BIOMIMETIC APPLICATION

ROBOTIC
EXOSKELETONS

Assisted living

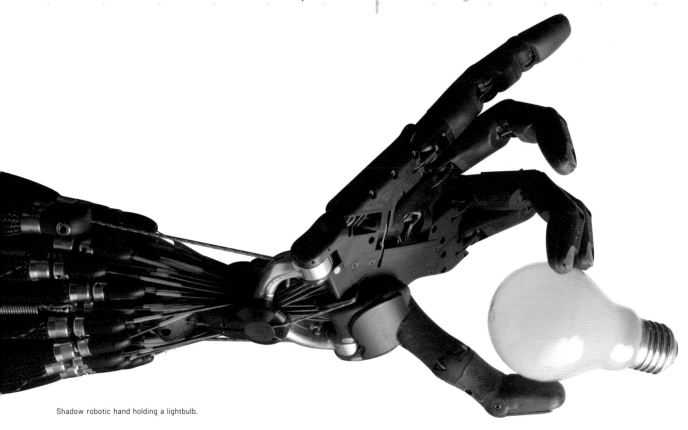

Shadow robotic hand holding a lightbulb.

Advances in medical implants and assistive devices, from hearing aids to pacemakers and bone and organ transplants, have given rise to an enormous global population of what are effectively man–machine hybrids. Our dependence on medical technology and its advances is part of the reason we are living longer and are more active at older ages than our ancestors, which makes this area of research critical to the future of social health and well-being. As medical devices and technology become more ubiquitous, the structures that reside outside the body will become more realistic in terms of morphology and functionality. User-centred design combined with robotic technologies drives the simulation of natural movement in such devices as the robotic hands designed and produced by, for example, the Open Hand Project and the Shadow Robot Company.

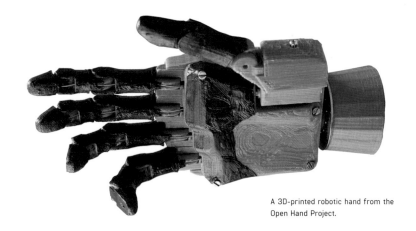

A 3D-printed robotic hand from the Open Hand Project.

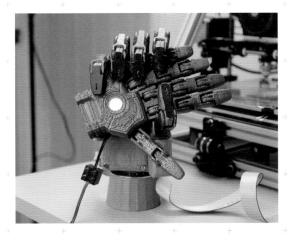

ABOVE, TOP AND RIGHT The Open Hand
Project made low-cost robotic prosthetic
hands with advanced dexterity using
emerging technologies such as 3D printing.
Their work is now being taken further by
Open Bionics.

BELOW The Shadow Dexterous Hand is a
robotic hand that demonstrates advanced
motor skills.

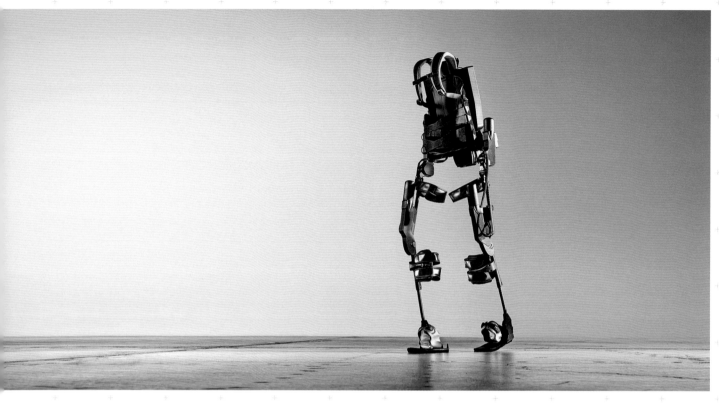

ABOVE The Ekso bionic exoskeleton before it is strapped on to a person.

OPPOSITE The Ekso bionic exoskeleton enables mobility for individuals who have lost functionality in their lower body.

RIGHT Prosthetic legs in which implantable sensing technologies enable the amputee to control the movement of the device subconsciously, by reading brain activity.

BIONIC SUIT

Ekso is one of the first commercial, wearable bionic suits designed as a biomedical device to enable individuals with lower-extremity weakness to stand and walk across conventional terrain with a natural, weight-bearing gait. Strapped over the patient's clothing, the suit forms an exoskeleton. As the user shifts his or her weight, sensors in the suit activate a mechanical device that initiates steps. The mechanism is driven by a series of battery motors that drive the legs and replace neuromuscular function.

The Ekso bionic suit can have a transformative impact on the lives of people with complete paralysis and minimal forearm strength as it enables them to stand and walk with a great degree of independence. It also functions as a gait-training device for rehabilitation of individuals with various levels of paralysis due to neurological conditions such as stroke and brain and spinal cord injury or disease.

Swifts (*Apus*) are remarkable aerial birds, among the fastest on the planet, which have evolved specialized wing structures that adapt their wing area and shape to allow optimum aerodynamic performance at different speeds and during manoeuvres. Swift wings are able to morph during flight by altering the angle between the wingtip and forelimb bones. The Wright brothers understood that if aeroplane wings could twist like those of a bird, manoeuvring would be simpler and more streamlined: this drove them to pioneer their wing-warping technology, incorporated into their first aeroplane in 1903.

OPPOSITE Swift wings can morph in flight, increasing the birds' ability to manoeuvre.

ABOVE Artist's rendering of NASA's vision for the aircraft of the future featuring morphing wings.

MORPHING WINGS

Aircraft wings are specially designed to deliver aerodynamic performance at specific speeds, but are fixed structures that do not adapt to different speeds and trajectories. A team of research scientists at Pennsylvania State University, USA, led by George Lesieutre, professor of aerospace engineering, set out to understand whether morphing wings could be used to improve efficiency and control the flight of future aircraft. Following an in-depth study of the role of swift wing sweep on aerodynamic performance, the group discovered that extended wings are most efficient during slow glides and turns and can generate lift, while swept wings are optimal

during fast glides and turns and can bear extreme loads. The findings of this study were applied to the development of a small-scale morphing aeroplane wing concept, which featured a cellular truss structure made from repeating diamond-shaped units connected with bendable shape memory alloys that function like tendons and manage shape change. The team designed a wing structure capable of adapting both area and cross-section shape to accommodate slow and fast flight requirements.

NASA's Dryden Flight Research Center at Edwards Air Force Base, California, is home to a new breed of supersonic jet aircraft. Drawing on the Wright brothers' approach and the work conducted at Penn State, a team of NASA

engineers in cooperation with the US Air Force Research Laboratory (AFRL) and Boeing Phantom Works has created the first aircraft with morphing wings. Active Aeroelastic Wing (AAW) is the experimental technology that enables deflection when special leading- and trailing-edge control surfaces are activated. The team behind this innovation envisions a new class of aircraft wing design that could replace stiff wings and heavy control surfaces. Although in its current format AAW relies on hinges for morphing behaviour, the idea is to replace these with strong, flexible composites able to bend during flight to achieve flight control just like a bird.

OCTOPUS

Soft dexterous limbs

SOFT ROBOTICS

Flexible conformable machines

Metals, alloys, tough plastics, wiring and motors constitute the portfolio of materials from which robots are made. High-performance, robust materials are necessary in many fields, especially in industrial applications like robotic arms for the assembly of automotive vehicles and other products. Biorobotics is a relatively new subsection of the robotic industry and as such has inherited the standard materials and construction methods. Biomimetic locomotion in random environments is one of the key objectives in biorobotic research: motion in nature requires flexible, agile, responsive materials such as muscle, while the inflexible nature of conventional robotic materials has created barriers in the engineering of devices able to transition smoothly from one state or position to another when exposed to irregular conditions. As a result, an exciting new field of soft robotics has evolved, which explores the development of responsive materials and structures that alter their properties in response to environmental stimuli such as electrical current, temperature, or presence of chemicals. It looks at their application in biomimetic robotic systems – for example, in underwater swimming robots composed partly of hard materials and partly of soft electroactive polymers that control the tail movement, similar to the muscles in a fish's tail.

ABOVE The wonderpus octopus has a distinctive pattern of white spots and stripes.

BELOW Close-up of octopus tentacle.

The days of big, rigid robots that sit in place and carry out the same repetitive task day in and day out are fading fast.

Don Ingber, Founding Director, Wyss Institute for Biologically Inspired Engineering, Harvard University

BELOW Detail of octopus tentacle.

BOTTOM RIGHT Close-up of octopus arms' suction cups.

RIGHT Illustration of octopus tentacle cross-section. The octopus body is completely soft yet its arms are capable of high dexterity. This is based on an arrangement whereby the muscle fibres are oriented in three different directions: along the axis of the arm, at a right angle to the axis, and wrapped diagonally around the axis. The antagonistic forces created between these muscles enable the arm to elongate, bend and shorten.

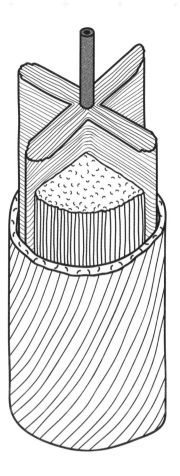

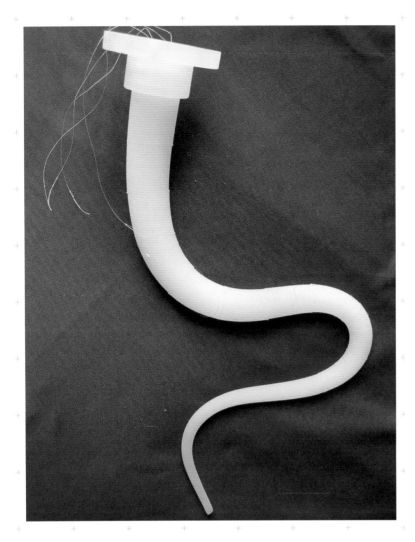

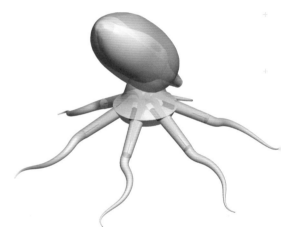

LEFT The PosieDRONE soft robotic tentacle prototype.

BELOW Artist's rendering of the PosieDRONE prototype.

OPPOSITE The PosieDRONE tentacle is able to wrap and grip.

POSEIDRONE

The octopus is a highly intelligent, soft-bodied invertebrate with long tentacles capable of incredibly accurate and sophisticated underwater behaviours in often confined and extreme environments. In 2009 a consortium of European researchers was awarded a grant to develop a biomimetic soft-bodied robot based on the morphology and behaviour of the octopus. The team developed a new technology platform including soft moving parts, synthetic skins with embedded sensors, and control architectures (a communication protocol for controlling devices within a network), which they applied to the construction of a soft robot capable of swimming,

crawling over irregular terrain, and complex handling tasks in extreme environments. The outcomes of this project formed the basis for PoseiDRONE, a spinout project that focuses on the creation of a self-contained robotic platform specifically designed for marine operations such as coastal and offshore engineering, petroleum and drilling technology, underwater archaeology and environmental protection.

The PoseiDRONE robot is composed of three units: a crawler, a swimmer and several manipulators. More than 76 per cent of its volume consists of soft elastomeric rubber; it weighs 0.755 kilograms (1.66 pounds) and features eight silicone arms each of which is 25 centimetres (10 inches) in length, while the whole

robot is 78 centimetres (30 inches) long. The first PoseiDRONE prototype is able to negotiate uneven and irregular environments similar to the ocean floor, and retrieve simple objects like a screwdriver using its arms. In its current form the prototype is capable of a limited range of performance when compared to its designers' ambitions for the final version, but forms an essential testbed for strategies and functions that will inform the design of the next iteration.

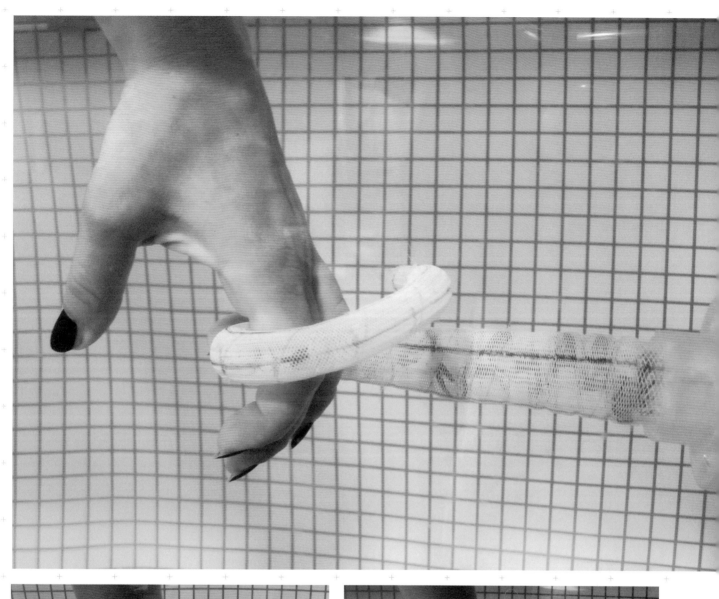

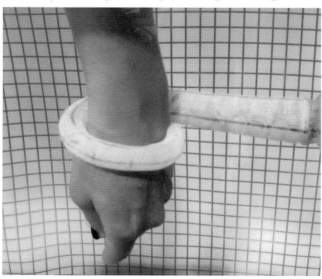

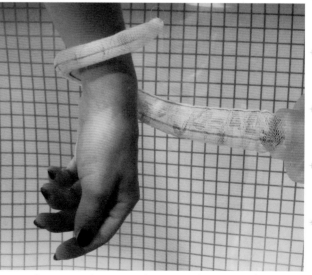

SELF-REPLICATION AND SELF-ASSEMBLY

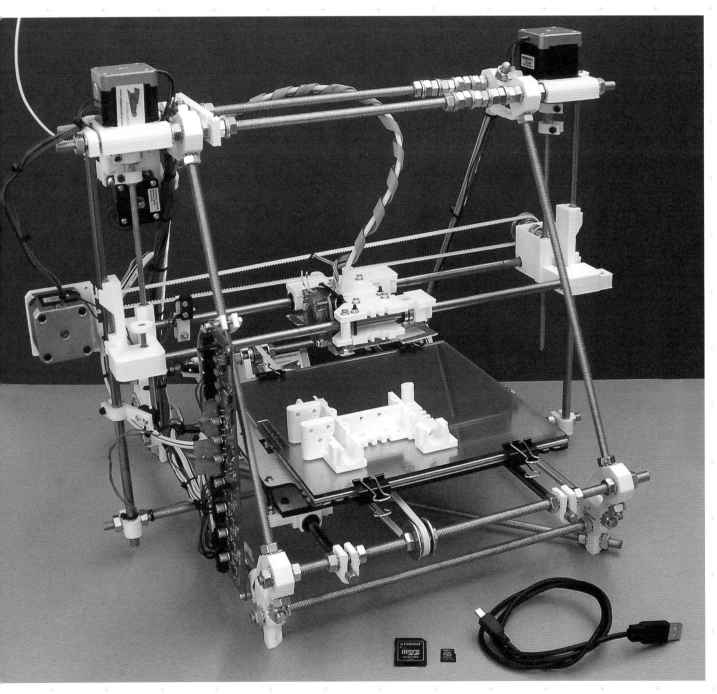

SELF-REPLICATION

Biological reproduction

REPRAP

Machines making machines

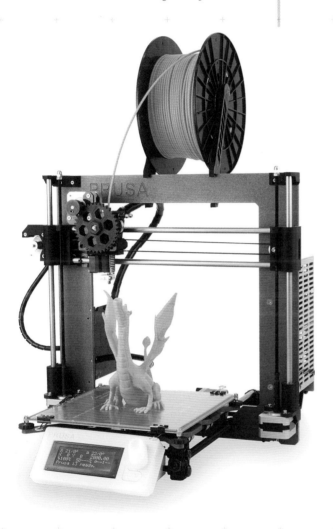

WHAT IF MACHINES COULD CREATE COPIES OF THEMSELVES?

In 2005, Dr Adrian Bowyer, a senior lecturer in mechanical engineering at the University of Bath, UK, founded RepRap (REPlicating RAPid prototyper), a project to create a 3D printer that can print its own components – in other words create a replica of itself. The aim of this project was to democratize access to 3D fused filament fabrication technology – the most popular form of 3D printers for amateur users – by creating cheap, reproducible machines for hobbyists, researchers and scientists, that operate using freely available software.

In 2005, a commercial printer created some of the original RepRap parts, while other parts such as structural bars and electronic components were externally sourced. In 2006, parts printed by the first RepRap prototype replaced those created by the commercial system. Since then, more and more of the machine's parts have become printable, including circuit boards. Most recently, the core team has focused on developing a system that enables cheap production of recycled printing filaments.

Since its conception, the RepRap project has exploded into a dynamic global effort attracting hundreds of collaborators, whose contributions have fuelled its evolution from a single design to numerous versions, each with distinct features and functionalities. The number of RepRap units produced by RepRap machines outside the lab remains unknown.

Several different RepRap models have evolved, including the Mendel (opposite), and the Prusa i3 (above). The Darwin (top right) was the original version. All the designs produced by the RepRap project have been released under an open software licence and are freely available for use and development.

One of the most fundamental features of life is the ability to procreate; all living organisms are the product of either sexual or asexual biological processes. Asexual reproduction (common in single-cell organisms, bacteria and several plants and fungi) involves an organism creating a copy (clone) of itself. Plant cloning is a well-established method in horticulture of cultivating species that have significant properties or commercial value such as grapes, potatoes and bananas. However, artificial cloning of animals and humans belongs to a controversial area of biotechnology subject to significant ethical debate. Human cloning of any kind is outlawed in many countries, although therapeutic cloning for medical purposes has been legalized in some parts of the world.

MOVEMENT

Plant and animal biomechanics

SCULPTING
WITH MOTION

From static to animated design

Movement is a fundamental ability demonstrated by plants and animals, essential to survival, that enables activities such as seeking food, reproducing, escaping predators and finding shelter. Physical mobility at organism level (rather than cellular or molecular) plays a significant role in the multifunctional and adaptive characteristics of living organisms. Could man-made products increase their functional and adaptive capacities if they were capable of movement?

RIGHT A Topobo Griffin walking model.

BELOW Detail of Topobo module.

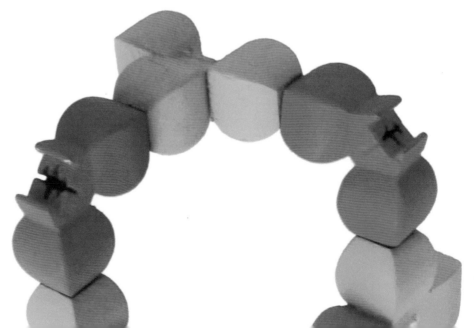

TOPOBO

Designers are not trained to work on products that will autonomously alter their structure; they are used to working on static applications rather than dynamic motion. In 2004 Amanda Parkes, Hayes Raffle and Professor Hiroshi Ishii at Massachusetts Institute of Technology (MIT) collaborated on a project to understand what it is like to 'sculpt with motion' in an attempt to challenge the status quo. The outcome of the work was the creation of Topobo, a modular, structural robotic system with 'kinetic memory' – able to record and play back physical motion. Individuals can build kinetic models simply by snapping together passive (static) and active (motorized) components; animation is introduced to the structure through physical manipulation of the parts by pushing, pulling and twisting. The active components record the action and play the motions back repeatedly. Topobo was designed as a teaching tool for non-experts, including children, to learn about dynamic structures, just as we learn about static structures by playing with building blocks. During many of the workshops the team conducted during the project, they found that Topobo enabled anyone to engineer locomotion into a structure, a feat that usually takes robotic scientists years to achieve.

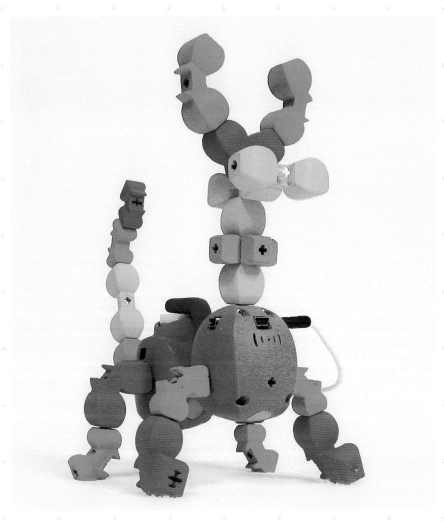

ABOVE A Topobo Moose model composed of multiple functional blocks, known as 'passives', which can be connected end-to-end or by their central notches.

LEFT Rear view of Topobo Walker model. The central 'active' module has a servo motor with a built-in position sensor.

BIOLOGY

PROTEIN
MOLECULES

Dynamic 3D folding

BIOMIMETIC APPLICATION

SELF-ASSEMBLING
FURNITURE

Active design

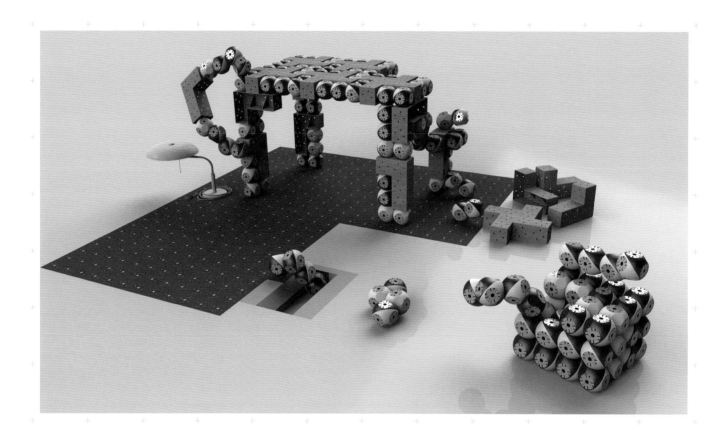

Roombots are simple, modular robots that
connect to form different structures.

Self-assembly is a process in which basic
components move from a disordered state
to an organized structure purely through
local interactions of components rather than
external direction. Materials and structures in
nature demonstrate self-assembly especially at
molecular scale. There are thousands of different
types of proteins in our bodies, each type
varying in function and properties depending
on its structure. These protein molecules are
able to recognize each other and connect
over and over again to make more complex
hierarchical structures such as supermolecules
(or supramolecules), organelles and cells.

SELF-ASSEMBLING
FURNITURE

Imagine if a collective of modular robots
could self-assemble autonomously to form
functional furniture, and furthermore was able
to reconfigure into a series of dynamic interior
fixtures and fittings depending on usage and
needs. The Biorobotics Laboratory at the École
Polytechnic Fédérale de Lausanne, Switzerland,
set out to invent just that. Roombots are modular
robots designed to be used as building blocks
for animated furniture able to self-assemble and
reconfigure autonomously.

The Roombot system consists of multiple
simple attachable and detachable robotic
modules with connectors that allow the creation
of dynamic structures such as tables, chairs,

sofas and beds. The team's vision is to create
furniture that will change location, shape and
function (for example a stool becoming a chair)
according to the user's needs. If left unused
over time, the modules go into 'sleep' mode and
create a static structure such as a wall or box.
Applications for this type of dynamic system
include assistive furniture for the elderly or those
with physical disabilities, reconfigurable public
spaces, and so on.

The group is currently working on
multifunctional and assistive robotic furniture
that can interact with elderly users to prevent
falls, monitor health and support transition from
one position to another (lying, sitting, standing),
as well as to move devices within the room,
bringing them closer to or further from the
user depending on need.

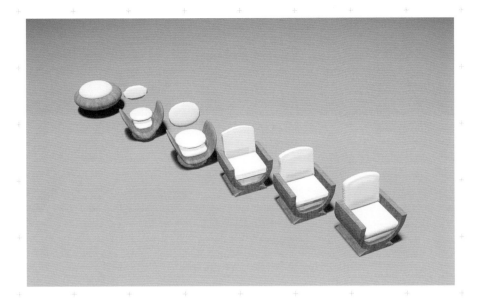

LEFT Artist's impression of morphing furniture concept.

BELOW The molecular structure of a protein molecule.

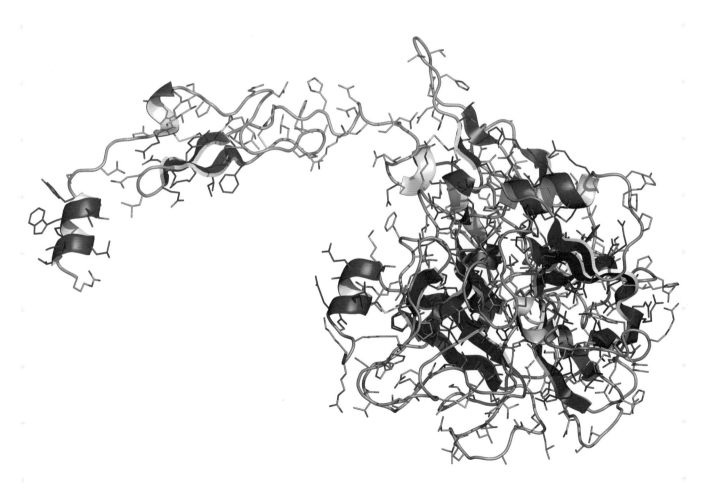

FLOWER BUDS

Deployable structures

AUTONOMOUS SELF-ASSEMBLING ROBOTS

Transitional design from two to three dimensions

A red poppy bud during bloom: after being tightly packed, the petals unfold.

One form of self-assembly in nature involves the way that buds unfold to reveal petals or leaves; similarly, linear sequences of amino acids fold into complex proteins with sophisticated properties. Inspired by such examples, engineers and computer scientists from Harvard's Wyss Institute for Biologically Inspired Engineering, the School of Engineering and Applied Sciences (SEAS) at Harvard, and the Massachusetts Institute of Technology (MIT) joined forces to create an autonomous self-folding device able to assemble itself from a flat sheet of material into a 3D robot that simply crawls away without any human intervention.

In just four minutes the robot created
by engineers from Harvard and MIT
assembles itself and crawls away.

SELF-ASSEMBLING ROBOTS

Adopting the principles of origami, the team arrived at the optimal folding design using computer design tools and dozens of prototypes. The thin composite sheet included a flexible circuit board in its centre and regions of polystyrene (a material that shrinks when heated) placed in strategic positions to function as hinges that realize the origami folding pattern;

two motors, batteries and a microcontroller were added. The polystyrene hinges contained embedded heating elements managed by the microcontroller.

The microcontroller triggers the heat elements, which causes the composite to self-fold in a series of steps. The hinges cool after a few minutes, and as the polystyrene hardens the robotic system stiffens into shape: at this point the microcontroller signals the robot to start crawling. The prototype achieved a speed of 160 metres per hour (540 feet per hour) and

consumed the energy of an AA battery. More recently, the team's MIT partners have created a micro version of this robot only 1 centimetre (0.4 inch) in length.

Self-assembly technology applied to large, complex structures such as robots is likely to play a significant role in the future of exploration and construction in hazardous environments both on Earth and in space. Flat-packed machines could be deployed to such environments and left to assemble themselves before setting out to perform specific tasks without endangering human life.

BELOW 4D-printed self-assembling strands from Skylar Tibbits' Self-Assembly Lab at MIT.

WHEAT AWN

Movement without muscle

AMORPHOUS ROBOTS

Non-mechanical machines

LEFT Artist's rendering of robotic wheat awn.

BELOW Multimaterial study by Hod Lipson of smart beams that bend in response to stimuli.

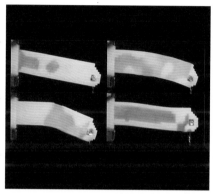

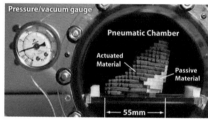

ABOVE Amorphous crawling robot by Hod Lipson in which locomotion is powered by changes in temperature.

In 2007 researchers from the Max Planck Institute of Colloids and Interfaces in Potsdam, Germany, discovered that individual grains of wild wheat have the ability to drill themselves into the soil. This remarkable behaviour is due to the design of two hairlike structures protruding from the grain known as awns. The external side of each awn is lined with tiny stiff hairs; the awns themselves have the ability to bend in dry conditions and straighten in damp. Repeated cycles of damp nights and dry days create a scissoring type of motion that helps propel the grain into the ground. The specialized hairs on the side of the awn prevent the structure from moving backwards, thus ensuring forward motion into the earth. Domesticated wheat has lost this self-propagating ability.

MATERIAL ROBOTS

Structures such as the wheat awn are inspiring a new class of robotic device: material robots. These are devices without batteries, motors, electronics or wires whose behaviour emerges from the sum of the materials from which they are made. These devices can draw on unconventional sources to power their mechanisms, such as moisture, temperature, chemical presence and pressure.

Hod Lipson, Professor of Mechanical Engineering at Columbia University, New York, is a visionary engineer and former leader of the Creative Machines Lab at Cornell University, Ithaca, New York. Lipson began using evolutionary algorithms to design

robots during his postdoctoral work, and his team at the Creative Machines Lab carried out several pioneering projects involving unusual approaches to robotic design and manufacture. In 2010, the team applied evolutionary algorithms to the design of a soft, amorphous 3D-printed robot that could move without any electronics. The outcome was a series of composite structures, composed of two types of polymers with different degrees of shrinkage when exposed to heat, that lacked any conventional components or moving parts typical of robotic structures. Instead, locomotion was achieved through the overall shape change of the device created by the shrinking and swelling between the two types of polymer during hot and cold environmental cycles engineered by the team.

PROGRAMMABLE MATERIALS

American designer and computer scientist Skylar Tibbits, originally trained as an architect, is the founder and director of MIT's Self-Assembly Lab, whose focus is on developing 'programmable materials' for the design and production of self-assembling products for the built environment. His vision is to shift from energy-rich manufacturing to a simple ambient paradigm that draws on passive energy such as temperature, pressure or moisture to power the assembly of products.

The Self-Assembly Lab has produced a series of programmable materials, including self-transforming carbon fibre, printed wood grain, and textile composites, that draw on environmental stimuli to self-transform. In 2013 Tibbits used the term '4D design' during a TED talk to describe the notion of designing with programmable materials, enabled by recent technology breakthroughs in multimaterial 3D printing and capability in simulation and optimization software.

The team has successfully programmed carbon fibre to transform autonomously. A heat-responsive material is printed on cured, flexible carbon fibre, making it change its shape when exposed to high temperatures, resulting in improved aerodynamic performance. This technology has been used for a morphing supercar wing explored in partnership with the Briggs Automotive Company (BAC) and engine flaps for Airbus.

The Self-Assembly Lab has also produced 'programmable wood' to be used as an alternative to traditional wood-bending techniques, thus avoiding the use of complex steaming and labour-intensive forming processes. Flat sheets of printed wood composite are designed to self-assemble into predetermined forms. The current prototypes use water to activate the shape change; Tibbits envisions a future where wood composites can adapt to extreme environmental conditions.

The group has also developed methods of printing layers of material of varying thicknesses on to stretched textiles, by which it is able to engineer morphing structures that assemble into pre-programmed shapes. The group believes that programmable textiles have potential applications in product manufacture, furniture, shipping (flat-pack, low-cost) and user interaction.

Skylar Tibbits and the team at MIT's Self-Assembly Lab designed programmable wood (opposite top and detail, below right), programmable carbon fibre (opposite bottom) and programmable textiles, which change their shape in response to environmental factors.

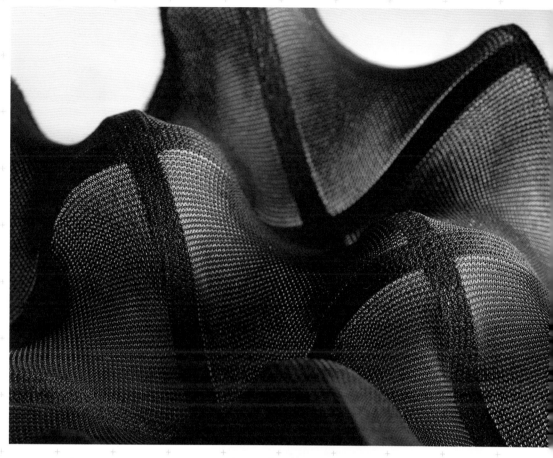

SELF-ASSEMBLING GARMENTS

Most materials in biology are programmed, from self-assembling amino-acid chains to seed pods. Information about how to react and under which conditions is embedded in the materials across a variety of scale from nano to micro to human. A simple experiment titled 'Loom to Hanger – Just Add Water' carried out in 2009 by a team led by Veronika Kapsali and supported by Julie Stephenson from the School of Art and Design at Middlesex University, UK, set out to program a flat woven textile to self-assemble into a 3D fully fashioned garment simply by exposing it to hot water, thus eliminating the need for additional processing such as cutting and sewing. The team combined the known effects of wool's shrinking when exposed to hot water with a hierarchical approach to the design of textiles to create a non-reversible 3D-engineered deformation. The resulting structure transforms a property in wool considered problematic into a self-assembling mechanism. It also demonstrates that a shift in thinking about materials can deliver a programmable structure that shifts from 3D to 4D design using conventional materials and traditional methods.

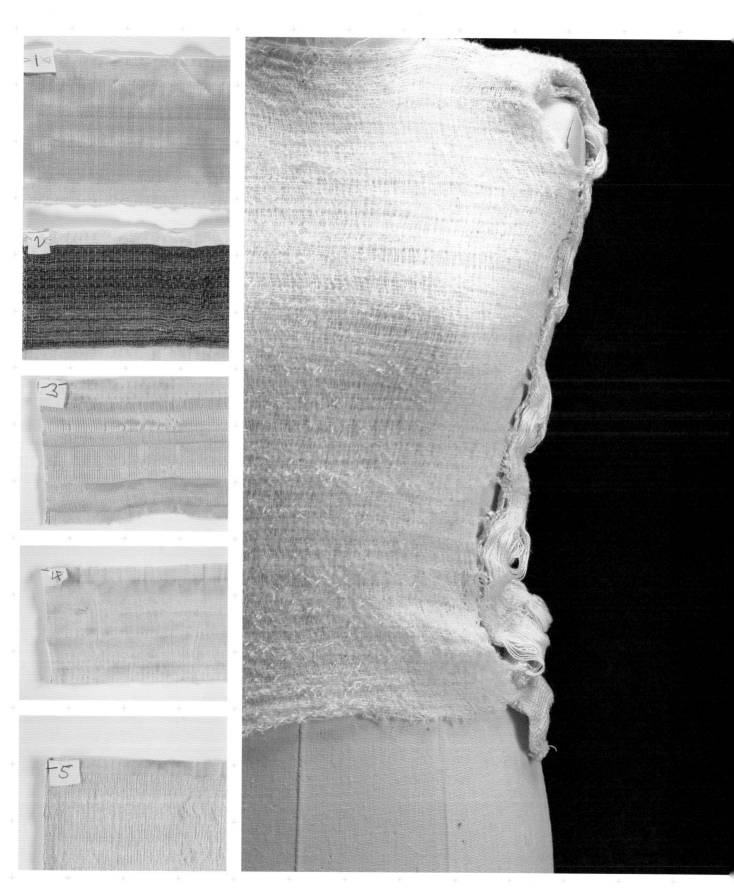

205

PENGUIN COAT

Multifunctional feather system

INSULATING TEXTILES

Variable geometry principle

King penguins swimming underwater, with (inset) a SEM detail of penguin feather at 800x magnification.

Penguins must withstand extreme cold during the Antarctic winter and be able to dive into freezing waters in order to feed. The penguin coat provides highly efficient insulation that minimizes heat loss through radiation and convection, with structural properties that function as an excellent wind barrier, eliminating heat loss through convection. Yet when the animal needs to dive for food, the coat transforms into a smooth and waterproof skin. This switch in functionality is achieved through a combination of motion generated by a muscle attached to the shaft of the feather and the clever design of the after-feather surface, which is covered in microscopic hooks that serve to control the direction of barb movement and prevent individual barbs from getting tangled as they are compressed and released. When the muscle is locked down the coat becomes a watertight barrier, and when released the coat transforms back into a thick air-filled windproof coat thanks to the guiding properties of the microscopic hooks. The air trapped in the layer created by the after-feather is partly released by the deliberate movement of the feather shaft, but some air remains in the coat, later to be released by the pressure created by the water as the animal travels through it. The release of air underwater creates a visible trail of micro-bubbles around the animal's body.

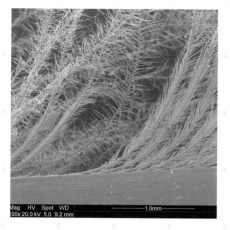  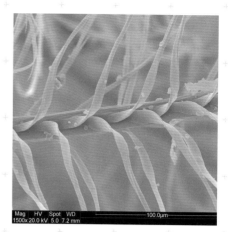

ABOVE SEM images of penguin feathers at varying magnifications: 1500x (left), 200x (centre) and 100x (right).

RIGHT Illustration of penguin afterfeather showing the microscopic hooks that control the direction of barb movement and prevent individual barbs from becoming tangled as they are compressed and released.

BELOW King penguins. The penguin coat is warm and insulating when dry, waterproof and streamlining when wet.

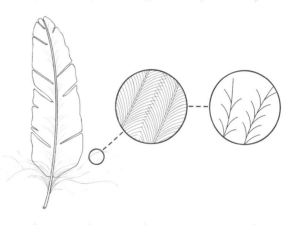

INSULATING TEXTILES

Attempts to interpret this mechanism into garments have led to the creation of an experimental textile system referred to as 'variable geometry'. The structure is made of two layers of fabric, which are joined together by strips of textile at a right angle to the plane of the two fabrics. By skewing the two parallel layers the volume of air between them reduces, resulting in the reduction of thermal resistance. The idea was used in the design of military uniform systems that can be adapted to function in both extreme cold and hot conditions. Gore & Associates created an ePTFE (polytetrafluoroethylene) membrane and polyester structures to be used as a garment insert under the brand name Airvantage, commercialized in 2002. The product allows the user to inflate and deflate the jacket, thus adjusting its insulation properties.

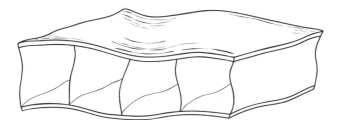

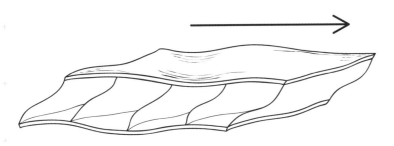

LEFT Illustration demonstrating variable geometry principle: two layers of fabric joined together by strips of textile perpendicular to the two fabrics. Reduction in thermal resistance is controlled by skewing the two parallel layers, reducing the volume of air between them.

BELOW Performance sleeveless jacket featuring variable geometry system.

OPPOSITE BMW motorrad jacket featuring inflatable lining.

PINE CONES

Hygroscopic seed dispersal

ADAPTIVE TEXTILES

Next generation moisture management

A pine cone in dry conditions – open (above) – and damp conditions – closed (above right). The cone opens and closes depending on the amount of moisture present in the atmosphere.

Plants are immobile structures without muscles, confined to a specific location for the duration of their lives. Paradoxically, in many species it is important that seeds travel as far away from the parent plant as possible to increase the chances of successful germination; effective dissemination strategies are therefore critical for survival. A diverse range of mechanisms has evolved to solve this problem, spanning from violent explosions to self-digging structures.

The most effective strategies involve waiting for optimal conditions before releasing seeds; these plants rely on specific environmental cues to trigger dissemination, such as atmospheric moisture content. Some species, such as pine, favour a dry climate for seed release, while others (usually desert species) wait for damp conditions. These plants use environmental moisture to power the dispersal mechanism, which is generally based on differential hygroscopic (relating to humidity) swelling between two adjacent areas of tissue.

In the early 1990s, Colin Dawson, part of the original Centre for Biomimetics at Reading University (see p.11) in the UK, analysed the hygroscopic opening and closing behaviour of cones from the pine, a coniferous evergreen of the *Pinophyta* family. Dawson found that the mechanism behind this behaviour was located in the pine-cone bract scales, which were composed of two different types of wood cell, both made from cellulose. He found that although both cell types absorbed similar amounts of moisture, they demonstrated very different swelling properties. Further investigation revealed that the amount of swelling was managed by the way in which the cellulose polymers were arranged in the cells; the cellulose chains in the non-swelling tissue were tightly packed together and oriented along the axis of the bract, while those in the swelling tissue had a looser configuration and were oriented at an angle to the bract axis.

The two types of tissue form a composite structure that resembles a bimetallic strip; the two types of wood cell change shape to different extents on contact with moisture. This difference creates an antagonistic force, which causes the bract to bend.

LEFT Maria Sharapova's Nike dress at the US Open, 2006. The loose sections engineered on the back curl out to allow skin moisture to evaporate.

BOTTOM LEFT Experimental jacket by Elena Manferdini for Nike.

BELOW Illustration of adaptive bilayer double-knit textile comprising a hygroscopic and a less hygroscopic layer. Slits create U-shaped flaps along the surface; these curl back when the hygroscopic layer is exposed to moisture.

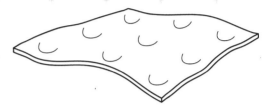

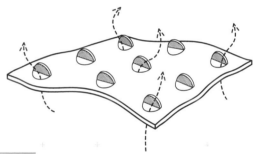

ADAPTIVE TEXTILES

Concentration of moisture within clothes is a key factor in the wearer's comfort; saturated air in a garment must be replaced by manual techniques. Hygroscopic swelling of fibres is considered a disadvantage in the textile sector. Dawson applied the insight he had gained from the study of pine cones to a textile system. Using a lightweight synthetic woven structure laminated on to a non-porous membrane, he created small U-shaped perforations in the surface that curled back when exposed to damp conditions and reverted in dry.

Nike implemented a similar concept in a clothing system. At the 2006 US Open, Russian tennis player Maria Sharapova wore a dress created from a double-knit textile comprising a hygroscopic layer next to the skin and a less hygroscopic layer on the outer surface, with engineered slits carefully positioned to aid microclimate ventilation. A fish-scale pattern on the back opened up as the athlete perspired to release perspiration and heat.

ABOVE Active INOTEK fibres shorten when
exposed to moisture; the image above
shows a sliver-knit textile with 100%
Inotek fibres in the pile. The surface of
the textile has been exposed to moisture,
causing fibres to contract and the pile to
become shorter.

OPPOSITE Knitted textile with INOTEK fibre
edge showing reversible shape change
when exposed to moisture.

AUTONOMOUS SELF-REGULATING TEXTILES

INOTEK is an award-winning biomimetic textile
technology that emerged from the pine-cone
work conducted by Colin Dawson, Julian Vincent
and George Jeronimidis in the 1990s. The project
had remained dormant from 1995 until 2005,
when Veronika Kapsali applied a novel design-
led approach to the project outcomes as part
of her doctoral work. The purpose of the work
was to engineer a commercially scalable textile
system that applies the mechanical shape-
changing principles of hygroscopic seed dispersal
mechanisms such as the pine cone to the design
of a fabric that would be able to alter its structure
and its ability to allow air to flow through it
depending on the microclimate conditions and
without any additional energy input.

INOTEK fibres are engineered to have a
natural curl in dry conditions; when exposed

to higher humidity the fibres become curlier,
and in so doing they shorten in length. Kapsali's
in-depth study into the way cellulose microfibril
orientation in wood cell walls can manage the
overall hygroscopic swelling direction of the cell
inspired the design of the INOTEK yarn. Active
fibres are positioned at an angle to the axis of
the yarn, directing the moisture-induced shape
change away from the length of the yarn and
focusing it to the width.

Textiles made from INOTEK demonstrate
counterintuitive behaviour. Conventional textile
fibres such as cotton, wool and rayon trap
moisture within their structures, causing them to
swell. As the fibres swell, the fabric yarns swell,
which in turn reduces the textile's ability to allow
air to pass through, a phenomenon directly linked
to physiological discomfort. INOTEK fabrics do
the opposite: the yarns become thinner, thus the
textile is more permeable to air, allowing it to
adapt its properties autonomously, depending
on the activity of the user.

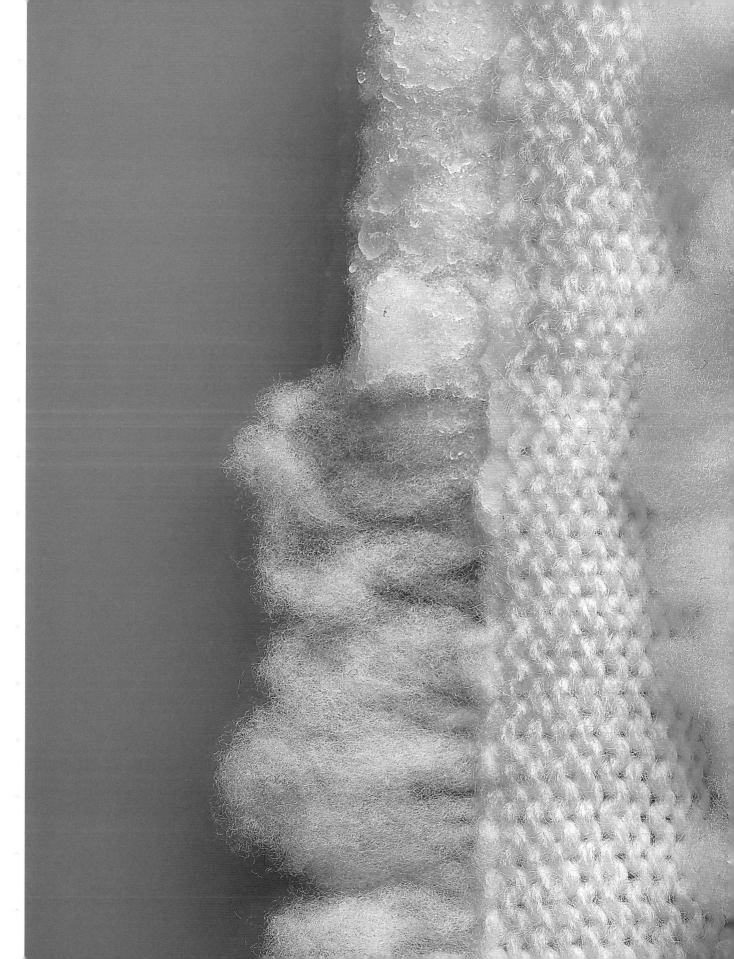

SPRUCE CONES

Moisture-responsive structures

PROGRAMMABLE WOOD

Hygroscopic ventilation

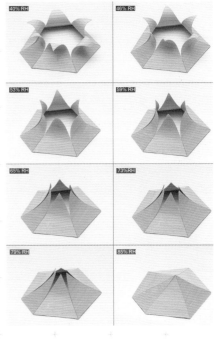

ABOVE HygroSkin (see p.216) – responsive component design.

LEFT Spruce cones – damp (closed) and dry (open).

BELOW HygroSkin – detail of responsive module closed and open.

The spruce – like the pine, part of the *Pinophyta* family – is another example of a cone-bearing tree. Spruce cones demonstrate the same inherent morphing behaviour as pine cones in the presence of moisture: cone bracts are opened when dry and closed when damp by means of the same hygroscopic principles (see p.210). These seed-bearing cones, an incredible example of climate-responsive systems, inspired architect Achim Menges, Professor of Computational Design at the University of Stuttgart, Germany, to create a climate-responsive architectural skin able to alter its shape passively by drawing on information and energy from the environment, rather than following the conventional approach that requires advanced sensors, motors, electrical components and an additional energy supply.

The HygroSkin Meteorosensitive Pavilion was a robotically fabricated modular construction. Stages in the robotic fabrication included setup (right), measuring (centre) and trimming (bottom right).

BELOW Detail of HygroSkin module construction.

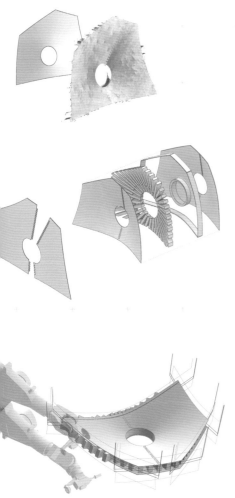

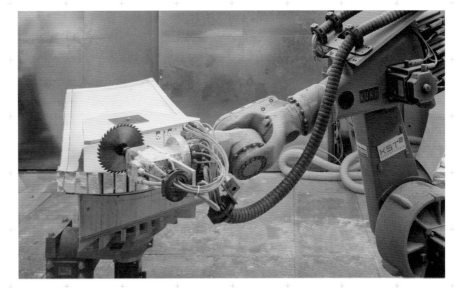

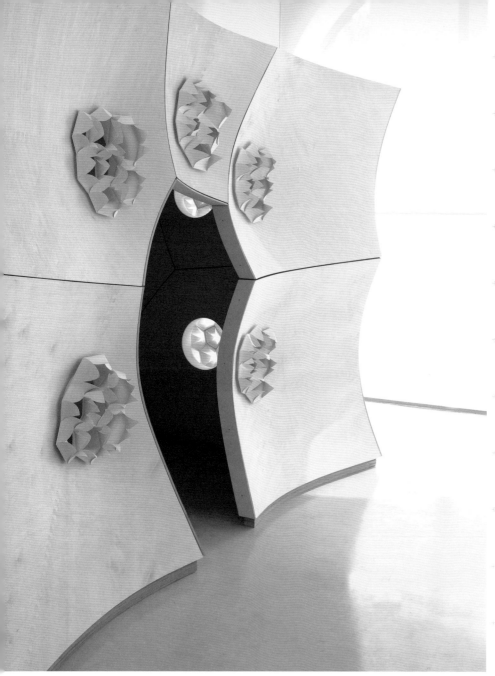

CLIMATE-RESPONSIVE WOOD

The HygroSkin Meteorosensitive Pavilion was made from carefully engineered fine plywood sheets that carried the load of the structure, featuring specially designed conical plywood composite units programmed to change shape – like a spruce-cone bract – in response to environmental humidity. By applying knowledge of the directional hygroscopic swelling properties of the plywood sheets strategically into the composite structure, Menges was able to recreate the bending motion demonstrated by the spruce cone. Each unit was able to autonomously alter its structure depending on the local microclimate, transforming the pavilion into a dynamic structure whose porosity, light transmission and visual permeability were in constant flux.

This visionary approach to design also results in the reinvention of the role of wood as a conventional construction material and transforms it into a climate-responsive natural composite. A biomimetic approach to design shows us that, as designers, we can create extraordinary structures from simple materials.

ABOVE Close-up of HygroSkin installation.

BELOW HygroSkin isometric drawing.

RIGHT ABOVE HygroSkin prototype.

RIGHT BELOW Structural analysis of prototype building.

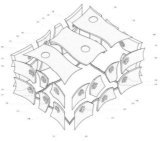

LEFT Detail of HygroSkin active module.

CENTRE LEFT Detail of interior view
of active module.

BOTTOM LEFT Interior view of
architectural skin.

BELOW Close-up of external view.

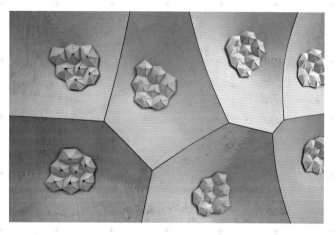

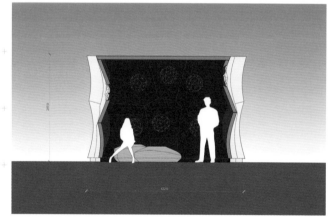

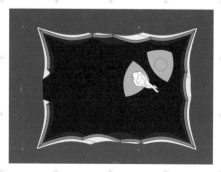

ABOVE (TWO ILLUSTRATIONS) Architect's
plan view (above) and section (above
centre) of the HygroSkin.

ABOVE The HygroSkin prototype structure on display at the FRAC Centre, Orléans, France, which commissioned the installation.

RIGHT Internal detail of active modules. Based on the functionality of the spruce cone, the flaps open and close autonomously depending on the amount of atmospheric moisture present.

ABOVE Detail of the HygroSkin installation at Orléans.

LEFT External detail of active modules.

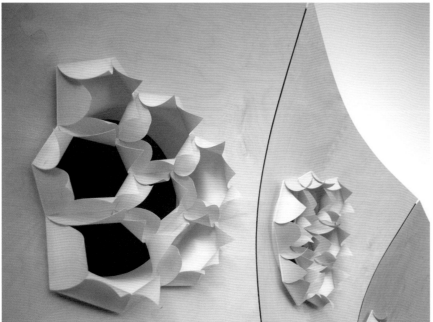

OCTOPUS SKIN

Active camouflage

DYNAMIC SOFT SURFACES

Advanced visual and textural display

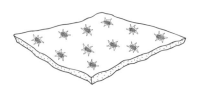

An octopus on a tropical reef (top) and a hooded cuttlefish (above): both animals have adapted their colouring so as to blend in with their surroundings.

ABOVE RIGHT Illustration of a chromatophore expanding (bottom) and contracting (top) to reveal or conceal a particular colour.

OPPOSITE Detail of a giant octopus.

Surface markings in animals have evolved to take on several important functions: for example, camouflage is used as a defence strategy. Markings can enable an animal to hide by blending in with its environment (zebra stripes, leopard spots), or to mimic the appearance of other species that are unattractive to a particular predator. Camouflage technology is important in military and surveillance operations, but conventional camouflage strategies are static, which means that pattern, colour and texture do not alter and need to be engineered specifically to a specific environment and season. Chameleons are iconic creatures known for their ability to mimic the colours and patterns of their surroundings, but they are not the only species that demonstrates remarkable dynamic skin coloration.

The skin of an octopus (a type of cephalopod) features by far the most sophisticated adaptive behaviour known to humans. The animals are able to transform their skin into soft conformable visual and textural displays, used not only to prevent detection but to intimidate predators and communicate with other cephalopods. The skin structure contains chromatophores (cells containing pigment) that can expand and contract to reveal or conceal a particular colour, like analogue pixels; these sit on layers of light-reflective tissue (iridophores) made from tiny sheets of reflective plates. The cephalopod is able to alter the colour reflected by the iridophores by changing the distance between the layers of reflective plate – this mechanism is controlled by a combination of hormones and the animal's nervous system.

OPPOSITE A traditional camouflage net made of green and grey material.

BELOW Soft, flexible polymeric material capable of responding to electrical stimuli designed by a team led by Xuanhe Zhao at MIT's Soft Active Materials Lab.

DYNAMIC SOFT SURFACES

In 2014, a team led by Xuanhe Zhao at Massachusetts Institute of Technology (MIT) unveiled a new, flexible, stretchable polymer able to alter both colour and texture in response to a change in voltage applied, based on the structure of the octopus skin. The team envisions obvious military applications for the new material, but the technology could also lead, for example, to a new form of flexible display screen.

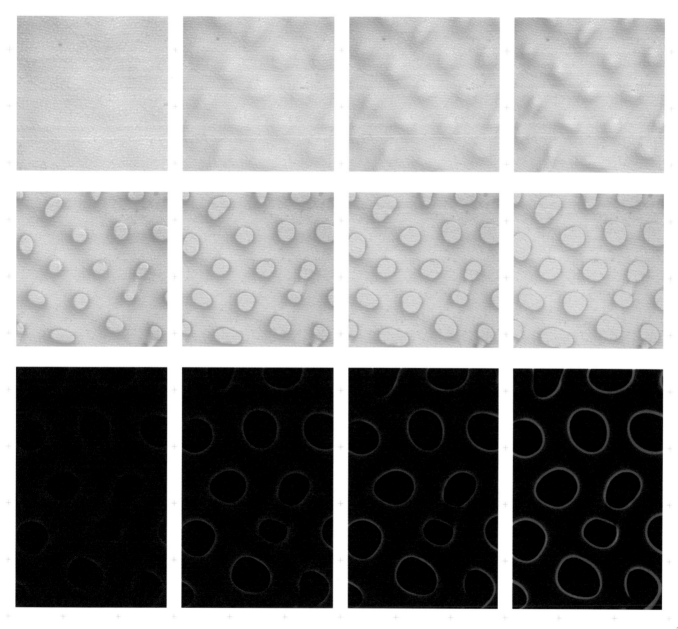

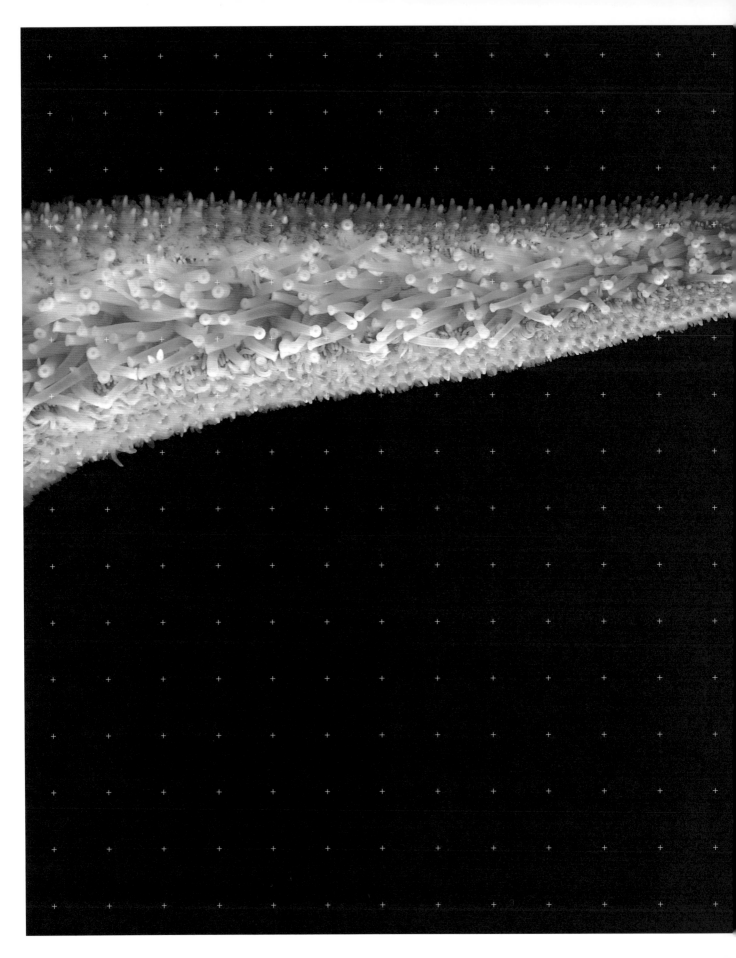

CONCLUSION

We are dealing with adaptive systems, probabilistic systems and systems closely integrated with their environment.

Otto Schmitt, Bionics Symposium, 1960

Otto Schmitt's vision extended beyond the limits of our existing thinking and technology; he proposed a new space of dynamic systems that link humans, products and the built environment within a symbiotic ecosystem. Since the first Bionics Symposium in 1960 (see p.11), biomimetic principles have been applied to many areas of engineering as well as to strategic thinking and business management. The clear alliance with sustainability and energy efficiency has made this approach attractive to numerous industrial and academic sectors, with some success stories in hand and many on the way. This book set out to provide a snapshot of the current state of the art in biomimetic developments that have most relevance to the design community in both the short and long term from the point of view of the design practitioner.

In 2006, a team of biomimetic researchers led by Professor Julian Vincent published a paper titled 'Biomimetics: its practice and theory' in the *Journal of the Royal Society Interface*. This article detailed a piece of work that explored the fundamental differences between technology and biology in their approach to solving problems. The team established a logical framework based on the mantra '*things* (substance and structure) *do things* (require energy and information) *somewhere* (space, time)'. Adapting a set of tools known as TRIZ (a Russian acronym meaning 'Theory of Inventive Problem Solving'), a system created in Russia to enable the translation of technical solutions from one field of engineering to another, they conducted a study analysing thousands of examples from both biology and engineering. The outcomes of the study revealed that there are significant differences between the way technical problems are solved in engineering and in biology. These were roughly quantified and illustrated according to scale, from nano to

Engineering TRIZ solutions arranged according to size/hierarchy

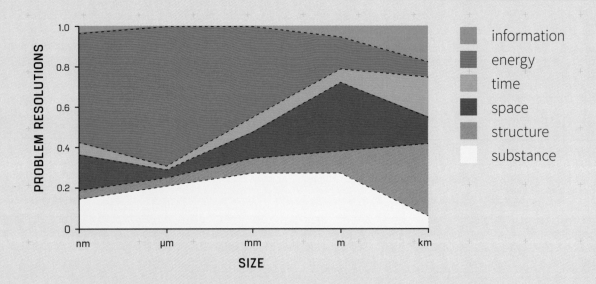

Biological effects arranged according to size/hierarchy

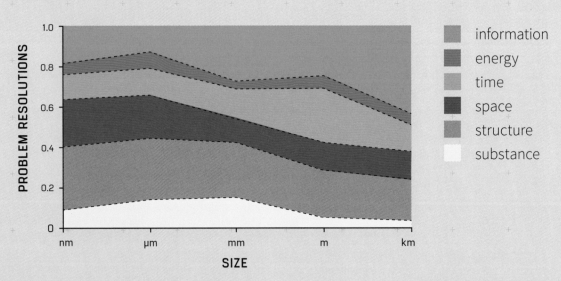

macro. The data were condensed into two graphs that give a graphic representation of the key differences in approach between making, designing or innovating in biology and in the man-made world.

Vincent contextualizes the study's findings by highlighting the sheer number of man-made polymers – currently exceeding 300 varieties – compared to the very few required by biology. The wide range of biological materials made from proteins (such as silk, muscle and enzymes) are made of similar monomers, yet the variety in emergent qualities and behaviour is not to do with the energy required to synthesize the materials but the way in which the basic building blocks (monomers) are arranged – which is, essentially, design.

In this book, the chapter titled 'Shape' offers examples of how morphology, even at human scale, can play a significant role in the performance or behaviour of an organism and how simple adaptations to the shape of a biological structure can deliver counterintuitive functionalities, essential to survival. The bumpy ridge of the humpback whale fin is a prime example of how design transforms a giant of the sea into an agile acrobat by harnessing the friction between animal surface and water to enable otherwise impossible levels of mobility. This chapter also begins to sketch out how properties and functionalities can be translated into our technological world, a process that is not exclusive to the trained mind of a scientist or scholar but is accessible to individuals who possess a grounding in a technical discipline such as wood- or metalwork and who are capable of intuitive processes of abstraction and synthesis.

The chapter titled 'Surface' explores the role of texture and how it can be applied to the creation of self-cleaning, antimicrobial, multifunctional surfaces. The aim of this chapter is to challenge the designer's perception of texture as a purely aesthetic or emotional factor and regard it as an opportunity to introduce additional functionalities through design. The skin of a shark, for example, is covered in microscopic, tooth-type structures made from skin (denticles) that feature a ribbed surface. As with the humpback whale, the morphology of the denticle manages the flow of water over the animal, enabling it to achieve great speed with little effort.

The chapter called 'Structure' aims to challenge our perceptions towards the role of material selection and introduces the notion of hierarchical design inspired by biology. As designers, engineers and makers, we rely on the properties of the materials we use to contribute mechanical and structural properties to our products; garments are made from soft, conformable textiles while buildings are made from strong, structural steel. We have the luxury of a wide portfolio of industrial materials to choose from – but the cost is ecological disaster. Biology offers a different approach, honed through a restricted palette. This chapter explores how design in nature is used to compensate. Cellular, honeycomb structures are made from simple and relatively weak materials, yet create resilient, strong structures. Designer Koji Sekita demonstrates that these principles apply across the scale, from molecular to human, with the creation of functional furniture using nothing but a few sheets of cardboard, cut and folded into modular, cellular structures. The design of individual cells can deliver counterintuitive properties, such as becoming fatter when stretched, rather than thinner.

Chapter 4, 'Making', introduces the notion of information-rich material systems (in biology) as opposed to those that are information-less (technology). In this context, 'information' means the instructions or guidance necessary to assemble a particular structure from a myriad of possibilities. This section also challenges traditional manufacturing methods that require someone or something to assemble components into a complex structure, often using vast amounts of energy and at great ethical and ecological cost, by exploring an alternative approach pioneered by advances in synthetic biology – especially, efforts to grow materials by feeding sugars and agricultural waste to micro-organisms, cultivating skin cells in mass at ambient conditions.

'Towards 4D' describes an emerging design space where information is embedded into the material of products to introduce spatial and temporal qualities to the system.

This chapter demonstrates how design coupled with material design can introduce an instruction into an object to be executed through physical processes without any external energy or effort; in other words, to alter the product's shape and physical properties for adaptation to changing external conditions or self-assembly. Skylar Tibbits' work applies this approach to the design of self-assembling furniture, while Hod Lipson creates 'robots without robotics' that do not require wires, batteries or computing and are capable of locomotion.

Our ability for analogical reasoning is what has enabled the transfer of properties, mechanisms and ideas from biology to technology. Shape, surface and structure are important factors in both creative and engineering design, as are materials and manufacturing. It has taken me the best part of nine years to realize that it is in fact the difference between the two graphs that signifies the opportunities for the creative sector: a biomimetic approach to design can offer a new perspective on the relationship between materiality, form and function, leading to a new design space that will in turn inspire a future where both graphs are more alike.

GLOSSARY

additive manufacturing (AM)
A method of building 3D objects by joining material together, usually layer by layer, using specialist devices such as 3D printers. Several technologies have been developed to manufacture products in this fashion, including stereolithography (STL), which uses high-precision lasers to cure photopolymers. Most consumer 3D printers use fuse deposition, which involves extruding plastic from the printer head.

amino acids
Organic compounds often serving as building blocks for proteins. An amino acid is formed by an amino group and a carboxylic acid group.

amoeba
A type of single-cell organism that has the ability to alter its shape, primarily by extending and retracting pseudopods (protrusions of the cell surface).

aramid (fibre)
Aromatic *polyamide*, a class of strong synthetic fibre. The molecules are aligned to the length of the fibre and strength is due to the strong chemical bonds formed between the molecules. Kevlar is a type of aramid fibre.

aspect ratio
The ratio between the lengths of the dimensions of a geometric shape (e.g. width to height).

bacteria
Prokaryotic (having no nucleus) microorganisms usually a few micrometres in length with a wide range of forms ranging from spheres to rods and spirals.

biofabrication
The use of cells, proteins, biological materials and *biomaterials* as building blocks to manufacture biological systems and/or therapeutic products.

biofouling
The accumulation of microorganisms, algae, plants or animals on wet surfaces such as boat hulls and other structures subject to long-term submersion in water.

biohackers
A community of non-institutional individuals experimenting with synthetic biology in makeshift labs.

biomaterial
A man-made substance engineered to interact with biological systems for medical or diagnostic purposes.

biopolymer
A *polymer* that occurs in living organisms, such as cellulose, protein and DNA.

biotechnology
The exploitation of biological processes for industrial and other purposes, such as the genetic manipulation of microorganisms for the production of medicine.

Boolean logic
A form of algebra in which all values are reduced to either TRUE or FALSE. Boolean logic is especially important for computer science because it fits nicely with the binary numbering system, in which each bit (basic unit of information in computing) has a value of either 1 or 0.

CAD (computer-aided design)
The use of computer systems and software to aid design in numerous fields, including architecture, electronics, engineering, manufacturing and prosthetics.

capillary action
Liquid flow in narrow spaces without the assistance of external forces and often in opposition to gravity.

chitin
A versatile natural long-chain *polymer* derived from glucose. Found in a wide range of biological organisms, such as the cell walls of fungi and the exoskeletons of arthropods and insects.

CNC (computer numerical control)
The computerized automation of machine tools. CNC machinery is designed to perform several carpentry tasks such as cutting and boring.

Cradle to Cradle
A biomimetic approach to the design of products and systems. Cradle to Cradle (C2C) is a registered trademark of McDonough Braungart Design Chemistry (MBDC) consultants.

cybernetics
Defined by its originator, American mathematician and philosopher Norbert Wiener, as 'the science of control and communications in the animal and machine' (Cybernetics, 1948).

drag
In fluid dynamics, a force acting opposite to the relative motion of any object moving through a surrounding fluid.

ductile
A material quality that allows the material to be stretched into a thin wire. Opposite of brittle.

elastomer
Another word for rubber, which can be made from natural and synthetic *polymers*.

EAP (electroactive polymer)
A *polymer* that changes its size or shape when exposed to an electrical field.

extrusion
A method of making composite materials by pushing them through a die. See also *pultrusion*.

filament (fibre)
A fibre of long continuous format. Wet- and melt-spun fibres are produced in filament form and can be thousands of metres long. The only natural filament fibre is silk, which can be more than 500 m (1,640 ft) long.

fusiform
A shape that is wider in the middle and tapering towards the ends.

heat convection
The transfer of heat from one place to another by the movement of liquids and gases.

helix
A three-dimensional spring-type shape, like a corkscrew.

hierarchical structure
A structure in which every entity in the organization except one is subordinate to a single other entity.

hydrophilic (surface)
A surface that is easily wetted by moisture vapour and water.

hydrophobic (surface)
A surface that does not allow moisture or water to adhere to or penetrate it.

hygroscopic
A substance able to retain water molecules from the environment through adsorption or absorption.

malleable
A material quality that allows the material to be flattened under compression.

microbe
Any type of organism that is not visible to the naked eye and can only be observed through a microscope lens.

microfibril
A very fine, fibre-like strand, or fibril, made up of glycoproteins (a type of protein) and cellulose.

micrograph
A photograph or digital image taken through a microscope.

micron
One-thousandth of a millimetre. Also known as a micrometre.

monomer
A molecule that may bind to other molecules to form a *polymer*.

nanofibre
A fibre with a diameter of less than 100 *nanometres*.

nanometre
One-billionth of a metre.

nanoparticle
A particle between 1 and 100 *nanometres* wide.

nanotechnology
The branch of technology that deals with dimensions of less than 100 *nanometres*; this mainly has to do with the manipulation of individual atoms and molecules.

natural fibres
Fibres that are naturally occurring in nature, usually from plants and animals, including cotton, flax, wool and silk.

neoprene
A composite textile consisting of a non-porous polyester membrane laminated on to a synthetic rubber and sandwiched between two layers of lightweight but tightly constructed textile.

newton
A unit of force named after Isaac Newton. One newton (N) is the force needed to accelerate 1 kilogram of mass at the rate of 1 metre per second squared.

peptide
A chain of *amino acid* molecules linked by covalent bonds (chemical bonds that involve the sharing of electron pairs between atoms).

permeability
The tendency of a material or structure to allow the passage of liquids and gases.

pneumatics
A branch of engineering that uses gas or pressurized air for actuation.

Poisson's ratio
When a material is compressed or extended in one direction it tends to expand or contract respectively in the other directions. The Poisson's ratio, ν (nu), is a measure of this effect expressed as the fraction (or per cent) of expansion divided by the fraction (or per cent) of compression.

polyamide
A very large molecule with repeating units linked by amide bonds (a type of compound). Examples include silk, wool and nylon.

polymer
A large molecule composed of many repeating subunits, or *monomers*.

psi (pound-force per square inch)
A unit of pressure or stress representing the amount of pressure caused by a pound of force applied to an area of 1 square inch.

pultrusion
A method of making composite materials by pulling them rather than pushing (*extrusion*).

quantum dot
A nano-scale crystal of semiconducting material.

regenerated fibres
Man-made fibres derived from natural *polymers* that have been broken down and reconstituted into continuous *filaments*, such as rayon from cellulose.

SEM
Scanning Electron Microscope – produces an image by scanning a sample with a beam of electrons. Such images can have a resolution of higher than 1 *nanometre*.

semiconductor
A substance that can conduct electricity under some conditions but not others, making it a good medium for the control of electrical current.

staple fibre
A fibre of short defined length; all natural fibres (except silk) are staple, while man-made fibres can be cut down into staple format.

superhydrophobic
Extremely hydrophobic, or water-repellent, so that water droplets form a sphere rather than flattening out, as seen in the lotus effect.

synthetic biology
Inderdisciplinary field of biology and engineering.

van de Waals forces
Short-range electrostatic attractive or repulsive forces between certain types of uncharged molecules or atomic groups. Individually extremely weak, but en masse capable of significant force.

viscosity
A measure of a fluid's resistance to flow caused by internal friction due to its molecular structure. A fluid with large viscosity resists motion.

wicking fibres
Fibres that demonstrate *capillary action*, usually made from polyester and featuring a characteristic 'Mickey Mouse ears' cross-section. The grooves engineered by this formation create tight spaces that enable capillary action.

FURTHER READING

Bar-Cohen, Yoseph, *Biomimetics: Biologically Inspired Technologies*,
CRC Press, 2005.

Benyus, Janine M., *Biomimicry*, William Morrow, 1997.

Gordon, James Edward, *The New Science of Strong Materials:
or Why You Don't Fall Through the Floor*, Penguin UK, 1991.

Hawken, Paul, Amory B. Lovins, and L. Hunter Lovins, *Natural Capitalism:
The Next Industrial Revolution*, Routledge, 2013.

McDonough, William, and Michael Braungart, *Cradle to Cradle:
Remaking the Way We Make Things*, Macmillan, 2010.

Mazzoleni, Ilaria, *Architecture Follows Nature-Biomimetic Principles
for Innovative Design*, vol. 2, CRC Press, 2013.

Thompson, D'Arcy Wentworth, *On Growth and Form*, Cambridge University
Press, 1942.

Vincent, Julian, *Structural Biomaterials*, Princeton University Press, 2012.

Vogel, Steven, *Cats' paws and catapults: Mechanical Worlds of Nature
and People*, WW Norton & Company, 2000.

Vogel, Steven, *Comparative Biomechanics: Life's Physical World*,
Princeton University Press, 2013.

Vogel, Steven, *Glimpses of Creatures in Their Physical Worlds*,
Princeton University Press, 2009.

Vogel, Steven, *Life's Devices: The Physical World of Animals and Plants*,
Princeton University Press, 1988.

Vogel, Steven, *Prime Mover: A Natural History of Muscle*, WW Norton
& Company, 2003.

Vogel, Steven, *The Life of a Leaf*, University of Chicago Press, 2012.

PICTURE CREDITS

a=above, **b**=below, **c**=centre, **d**=detail,
l=left, **r**=right, **g**=background, **f**=foreground

2 Dmitry Grigoriev/Shutterstock; **6l** Nigel French/Shutterstock; **6r** Hendroh/ Shutterstock; **7** Momente/Shutterstock; **8a** Steve Mann; **8b** Muse™; **9** Peteri/ Shutterstock; **10a** Martin Caidin; **10b** Pan Xunbin/Shutterstock; **11a** Air Force Office of Scientific Research (AFOSR); **11b** Photowind/Shutterstock; **12a** Nicku/Shutterstock; **12b** Morphart Creation/Shutterstock; **13a** Wilm Ihlenfeld/Shutterstock; **13b** Zvonimir Atletic/Shutterstock; **14a** Korionov/ Shutterstock; **14b** Mrs_ya/Shutterstock; **15a** ONiONA/Shutterstock; **15bl, 15br** Anna Dimitriu: **16** Doctor Jools/Shutterstock; **17a** JD Photograph/ Shutterstock; **17b, 19** Whitehoune/ Shutterstock; **18** silkwayrain/istock by Getty Images; **20–21** mexrix/Shutterstock; **23** Mr Suttipon Yakham/ Shutterstock; **24a** Anna Krasovskaya/Shutterstock; **24b, 28a** Everett Historical/Shutterstock; **25** Kwanjitr/Shutterstock; **26l** Quayside/ Shutterstock; **26r** Ana Gram/Shutterstock; **27al, 27b** TonLammerts/ Shutterstock; **27ar** Tobias Arhelger/Shutterstock; **28b** Begood/Shutterstock; **29a** Photogal/Shutterstock **29b** Benoit Daoust/Shutterstock; **30a** Eric Isselee/Shutterstock; **30b** Alexandra Lande/Shutterstock; **31al, 31ar** Otto Lilienthal Museum; **31b** tea maeklong/Shutterstock; **32a** CLS Design/ Shutterstock; **32l** Mr Suttipon Yakham/Shutterstock; **32r** Bonnie Taylor Barry/Shutterstock; **33a** Policas/Shutterstock; **33b** Kangshutters/ Shutterstock; **34a** Dreamnikon/Shutterstock; **34b** QiuJu Song/Shutterstock; **35** WorldPictures/Shutterstock; **36** Butterfly Hunter/Shutterstock; **37** Anna Wilson; **38a** Willyam Bradberry/Shutterstock; **38b** Gerald Marella/ Shutterstock; **39a** http://www.dt.navy.mil/div/about/galleries/gallery3/054. html; **39b** Anna Wilson; **40a** Volt Collection/Shutterstock; **40b** David Ashley/ Shutterstock; **41al** Corlaffra/Shutterstock; **41ar** Pedrosala/Shutterstock; **41b** Anna Wilson; **42** Tory Kallman/ Shutterstock.com; **43** Roy Stuart; **44** Dray van Beeck/Shutterstock; **45a** Alex Wong/Getty Images; **45b** Timothy E. Higginbotham, Ph. D; **46–47** pixbox77/Shutterstock; **49** Eric Isselee/ Shutterstock; **50g** stockpix4u/Shutterstock; **50f** Alex Hyde/Science Photo Library; **51** S. Pytel/Shutterstock; **52l** Anna Wilson; **52r** Pascal Goetgheluck/ Science Photo Library; **52b** Airbus, Fraunhofer-Gesellschaft; **53a** Johan Swanepoel/Shutterstock; **53b** Holbox/Shutterstock; **54l** Gucio_55/ Shutterstock; **54r** Julie Lucht/Shutterstock; **55a** Fotokostic/Shutterstock; **55b** Joris van den Heuvel/Shutterstock; **56al** Svetlana55/Shutterstock; **56ar** Anna Wilson; **56b** Fotokostic/Shutterstock; **57a** Alekcey/Shutterstock; **57b** Marekuliasz/Shutterstock; **58l** Papa Bravo/Shutterstock; **58r** Aggie 11/ Shutterstock **59l** Leo Caillard; **59b** Anna Wilson; **59r, 60a, 60c, 61bl, 61br** UAmhersM: **60b, 61a** Eric Isselee/Shutterstock; **62** Siriwat Wongchana/ Shutterstock; **63** Ted Kinsman/Science Photo Library; **64a** Anna Wilson; **64c** Sto AG; **64b** Fnp/Shutterstock; **65** Leo Caillard: **66l** Jiri Hodecek/ Shutterstock; **66r** jps/Shutterstock; **67a** Anna Wilson; **67b** Peter Schwarz/ Shutterstock; **68l** Ossobuko/Shutterstock; **68r** Donna Sgro; **69a** iLight photo/Shutterstock; **69b** Sergei Aleshin/ Shutterstock; **70al** Beth Swanson/ Shutterstock; **70ar, 71br** scubaluna/Shutterstock; **70b** Anna Wilson; **71a** Veronika Kapsali; **71bl** Simon Leigh; **72a** Jubal Harshaw/Shutterstock; **72b** Anna Wilson; **73** Pan Xunbin/Shutterstock; **74** Leo Caillard; **75a** Jubal Harshaw/Shutterstock; **75b** Veronika Kapsali; **76l** Kristian Bell/Shutterstock; **76r** Anna Wilson; **77** Johanna Ralph/Shutterstock; **78** Martin Harvey/Getty Images; **79** Fogquest; **80** Leo Caillard; **81a** Anna Wilson; **81b** mkos83/iStock; **82** Robert Eastman/Shutterstock; **85a** Joe Gough/Shutterstock; **85b** Efired/ Shutterstock; **86d** Marc Poveda/Shutterstock; **86g** Michael Hero/ Shutterstock; **87al** Anna Wilson; **87bl** Institute of Textile Technology and Process Engineering Denkendorf; **87ar** Claudio Divizia/Shutterstock; **87** NYS/Shutterstock; **88** Jubal Harshaw/Shutterstock; **89** Claudio Divizia/ Shutterstock; **90l** Shaiith/Shutterstock; **90r** Dionisvera/Shutterstock;

91 Cesarz/Shutterstock; **92a** Michelin/Shutterstock; **92b** Hankook; **93** Bridgstone; **94, 95a, 95b** Leo Caillard; **96** zimowa /Shutterstock; **97a, 97c, 97b** Koji Sekita; **98a** s-ts/Shutterstock; **98b, 99a, 99b** Lilian van Daal; **100a** Graphic design/Shutterstock; **100b** Anna Wilson; **101a, c, b** Andy Alderson; **102** Jose Luis Calvo/Shutterstock; **103a** Anna Wilson; **103b** Andy Alderson; **104l** FatManPhoto/Shutterstock; **104ar** Orhan Cam/Shutterstock; **104br** Anna Wilson; **105a, b** Claudio Divizia/Shutterstock; **106** Bronwyn Photo/Shutterstock; **107al, r** Leo Caillard; **107b** julien.sebastien.jeremy/ Shutterstock; **108a** Zeng Wei Jun/Shutterstock; **108b** Fat Jackey/ Shutterstock; **109a** Eye of Science/Science Photo Library; **109b** Anna Wilson 110 Kazakov Maksim/Shutterstock; **111a, b** Anna Wilson; **112** Andres Warén; **113a** Oleksandr Pereplytsia/iStock; **113b** Anna Wilson; **114l** bluehand/ Shutterstock; **114r, 115b** Anna Wilson; **115a** BulentGrp/iStock; **116l, 116r, 117r** Dmitry Grigoriev/Shutterstock; **117la, b** Anna Wilson; **118l** outdoorsman/Shutterstock; **118r** Institute of Textile Technology and Process Engineering Denkendorf; **119a** Leo Caillard; **119b** Lex20/iStock; 120 aptecha/Shutterstock; **121a** showcake/Shutterstock; **121b** Anna Wilson; **122–123** Kirsanov Valeriy Vladimirovich/Shutterstock**; 124** Yermolov/ Shutterstock; **125** Pick/Shutterstock; **126a** John P. Ashmore/Shutterstock; **126b** AzriSuratmin/Shutterstock; **127a, b** Freedom of Creation; **128a** hxdyl/ Shutterstock; **128b** Anest/Shutterstock; **129a** Schankz/Shutterstock; **129b** Freedom of creation 130 Christopher May/Shutterstock; **131d** Jose Angel Astor Rocha/Shutterstock; **131g** Npine/Shutterstock; **131b** Everett Historical/Shutterstock; **132a** hxdbzxy/Shutterstock; **132b** Dmitry Naumov/ Shutterstock; **133al** Marsan/Shutterstock; **133ar** Noppharat46/ Shutterstock; **133b** Karel Gallas/Shutterstock; **134** Steve Gschmeissner/ Science Photo Library; **135a** sunipix55/Shutterstock; **135c** Pok Leh/ Shutterstock; **135b** cpaulfell/Shutterstock; **136l** Adrian Dennis/Getty Images; **136r** The Sun photo/Shutterstock; **137a** martin81/Shutterstock; **137bl** leshik/Shutterstock; **137br** Ekarin Apirakthanakorn/Shutterstock; 138 KuLouKu/Shutterstock; **139l** Bolt Threads; **139r** Humannet/ Shutterstock; **140** Pan Xunbin/Shutterstock; **141a** Chubykin Arkady/ Shutterstock; **141b** Ammit Jack/Shutterstock; **142a, 143al, ar, b, 144a, c, b, 145** Biocouture; **142b** Princessdlaf/iStock; **146** Kichigin/Shutterstock; **147a** Varin Jindawong/Shutterstock; **147b** Leo Caillard; **148, 149a, 150, 151** Amy Congdon; **149b** Kirill Demchenko/Shutterstock; **152d** Alan John Lander Phillips/iStock; **152g** pashabo/Shutterstock.com; **153a** Jubal Harshaw/Shutterstock; **153b** Muskoka Stock Photos/Shutterstock; **154a** GrayMark/Shutterstock; **154b** science photo/Shutterstock; **155ar** Susana Cámara Leret; **155** Mike Thompson; **156** Chatsuda Sakdapetsiri/ Shutterstock; **157, 158l** Veronika Kapsali; **158r** Dr Morley Read/ Shutterstock; **159a** sitboaf/Shutterstock; **159al** KimOsterhout/iStock; **159b** D. Kucharski K. Kucharska/Shutterstock; **160–161** Leo Caillard; **163** Kristina Vackova/Shutterstock; **164** Aleksandrs Marinicevs/ Shutterstock; **165al** kiri11/Shutterstock; **165bl** beerlogoff/Shutterstock; **165r** holbox/Shutterstock; **166, 168** NinaM/Shutterstock; **167** Sony; **169** Jose Luis Calvo/Shutterstock; **170a** Khoroshunova Olga/Shutterstock; **170b** Ilca Laurentiu Daniel/Shutterstock; **171** Travel mania/Shutterstock; **172** Self Organising Systems Research Group/Harvard University; **173al, ar, c, b** Clive van Heerden, Jack Mama together with Bart Hess, Nancy Tilbury, Peter Gal and Harm Rensink; **174–5** DLR Institute of Robotics and Mechatronics; **176** biorobotics lab EPFL; **177a** Robert Mandel/ Shutterstock; **177bl** SEAS; **177br** Konrad Mostert/Shutterstock; **178** foto76/ Shutterstock; **179ar, br, l, 180, 181a, b** Plantoid Project 2012; **182a, 183b** Shadow Robot Company; **182b, 183al, ar** Openbionics; **183a, 184a, b** Ekso Bionics; **183b** Vereshchagin Dmitry/Shutterstock; **186** Andrew Howe/iStock; **187** NASA National Aeronautics and Space Administration; **189a** Aquapix/ Shutterstock; **189b** Stasis Photo/Shutterstock; **190al** QiuJu Song/

ACKNOWLEDGMENTS

Shutterstock; **190ar** Anna Wilson; **190b** olgaman/Shutterstock; **190al, ar, 191a, bl, br** octopus-project-eu; **192, 193l, r** REP-RAP Adrian Bower; **194a, b, 195a, b** TOPOBO; **196** Biorobotics Laboratory Biorob EPFL; **197a** Leo Caillard; **197b** Molekuul/iStock; **198** Ernst W. Breisacher/iStock; **199** S.Felton Harvard University; **200, 202a, b, 203a, b** Skylar Tibbits/MIT; **201l** Leo Caillard; **201ar, br** Hod Lipson; **204, 205, 206d, 207a** Veronika Kapsali; **206g** Volt Collection/Shutterstock; **207b** Tom K Photo/Shutterstock; **207c, 208, 211r, 220ar** Anna Wilson; **208r** Aerostich; **209** Gore-tex; **210r, l** Sergiy Kuzmin/Shutterstock; **211a** Caryn Levy/Getty Images; **211b** Elena Manfradini for Nike; **212, 213** MMT Textiles Ltd; **214–219** Archim Mendes; **220a** NaturePhoto/Shutterstock; **220b** Cigdem Sean Cooper/Shutterstock; **222l** Dieter Hawlan/Shutterstock; **222** Lanych/Shutterstock; **223** Xuanhe Zahao; **224–225** AMA/Shutterstock; **228** Royal Society

I would like to thank Professor Julian Vincent for his patience and mentorship, and George Jeronimidis, Roger Turner, Barbara Mazzolai, Alessio Mondini, Hod Lipson, Jon Hiller, Adrian Bower, Andrew Alderson, Auke Ijspeert, Chris Nieckar, Francesco Giorgio-Serchi, Gregory Cossweiler, Jack Mama, John Stefanakis, Simon Leigh, Steve Mann, Oliver David Krieg, Michele Dragoescu, Martina Ohle, Thomas Stegmaier, Wolfgang Reinert, Achim Menges, Clive van Heerden, Donna Sgro, Elena Manferdini, Anna Dumitriu, Koji Sekita, Lilian van Daal, Mike Thompson, Roy Stuart, Susanne Lee, Amy Congdon for their ongoing support and inspirational work in this field.

A special thanks to Leo Caillard and Anna Wilson for creating amazing images; also to Gail Steckler, Andres Warén and Sally Pellow.

A very special thanks to Marion Lean for her assistance in this project.

INDEX

This book is dedicated to Poppy, Phoebe and Mark

Dr Veronika Kapsali is a Reader in Materials Technology
and Design at the London College of Fashion, University
of the Arts London; a Leadership Fellow of the Arts and
Humanities Research Council; and co-founder of MMT
Textiles Ltd. She is a leader in the newly emerging field
of bio-inspired textiles and has worked for over a decade
on a range of industry-focused applications, including
the invention and development of biomimetic active fibres
and textiles.

On the cover:
Front, clockwise from top left: Fat Jackey/Shutterstock, p. 108; Jubal Harshaw/
Shutterstock, p. 75; Leo Caillard, p. 74; Jubal Harshaw/Shutterstock, p. 72
Spine: images repeated from front cover
Back, top row, left to right: Ted Kinsman/Science Photo Library, p. 63;
Eric Isselee/Shutterstock, p. 49; Dmitry Grigoriev/Shutterstock, p. 116
Back, bottom row, left to right: Veronika Kapsali, p. 157; Efired/Shutterstock,
p. 85; Pedrosala/Shutterstock, p. 41

First published in the United Kingdom in 2016 by
Thames & Hudson Ltd, 181A High Holborn, London WC1V 7QX

First paperback edition published in 2021

Reprinted 2023

Biomimetics for Designers © 2016 Thames & Hudson Ltd, London

Text © 2016 Veronika Kapsali

Designed by Draught Associates

British Library Cataloguing-in-Publication Data
A catalogue record for this book is available from the British Library

ISBN 978-0-500-29638-7

Printed in and bound China, by Artron Art (Group) Co., Ltd.

Be the first to know about our new releases,
exclusive content and author events by visiting
thamesandhudson.com
thamesandhudsonusa.com
thamesandhudson.com.au